Praise for *Let's Put the C in PLC*

"Dr. Dumas thoroughly understands how to help others create a Professional Learning Community. His experience and work to implement this effective school culture was commendable and exceptional. This book is a synthesis of all he has *"learned by doing."* Leaders at all levels will do well to study and use this resource as they strive to improve the learning culture of their school."
— Craig Kautz, *retired Superintendent of district with multiple National Model PLC schools*

"As a secondary principal for the past 24 years, one of the most difficult aspects has been trying to get teachers to collaborate. It is not that they do not want to, it is that at the secondary level there are so many nuisances that make it difficult. Dr. Chad Dumas helps guide principals' leadership skills in making this task manageable and provides strategies to create your school into a perfect example of how a PLC can and should work to guarantee all students learn." — Brian Carico, *high school Principal*

"Leaders know all too well the daily challenges of competing district and school priorities, long lists of tasks to be completed, the limited resource of time, and are continually asking, 'How can we improve?' and 'How can we do better?' This book is written for school leaders like you!" — Scott Blum, *Director of Professional Learning*

"For leaders who genuinely desire to create a team of staff, parents and administrators working together toward common aims, this is your book. Dr. Dumas has successfully implemented what you will read. He is an expert, with great on-the-ground, K-12 successful experience." — Lee Jenkins, Ph.D., *author of* How to Create a Perfect School *and* Optimize Your School

"The idea of professional learning communities and learning teams offers great promise. Research and best practice have shown when teachers work collectively, focus their learning on their students' learning needs, and assess the impact of that learning, their students benefit. In his book, Chad Dumas makes the important point that building principals have a key role to play in creating the conditions needed for learning teams to thrive. Dumas also reminds us that it's not charisma but a principal's understanding of the key tenets of adult learning and cycles of continuous improvement that matter most. This practical guide will help school leaders and their leadership teams as they support the growth and development of their teachers and educator learning teams. Dr. Dumas, thank you for bringing this great resource to the field!" — *Frederick Brown, Chief Learning Officer, Deputy, Learning Forward*

"In *Let's Put the C in PLC*, Dr. Chad Dumas shines a spotlight on the specific knowledge school leaders need in order to build collective capacity for improvement. In this practical guide to the key priorities for leaders, Dumas highlights the key findings from the latest research as well as the perennial classics. Building on his award-winning dissertation, Dr. Dumas issues a call to action for leaders committed to turning their schools into true professional learning communities. Highly recommended." — *Justin Baeder, PhD, Director, The Principal Center and author of Now We're Talking! 21 Days to High-Performance Instructional Leadership*

"Leadership matters! It is not easy and can be lonely. It is rewarding and makes a difference! This book will make it easier, less lonely, more rewarding, and will amplify the difference that you make as you build a culture where 'we can do anything together.'" — *Mike Teahon, retired Superintendent and university Department Chair*

"Dr. Dumas clearly expresses the needs of our time to serve EVERY child through equitable learning environments. He provides practical tools and insights for school leaders to make this happen. Leaders who put these collaborative practices to use will ensure that persistent gaps are closed and all students reach their full personal and academic potential." — *Anthony Jones, Director of Equity*

Let's Put the C in PLC

Let's Put the C in PLC

A Practical Guide for School Leaders

Chad Dumas, Ed.D.

Foreword by Todd Whitaker

Copyright © 2020 by Chad Dumas

All rights reserved under the Pan-American and International Copyright Conventions. This book may not be reproduced, in whole or in part, in any form or by any means, electronic or mechanical, including photocopying, recording, or by any information storage and retrieval system now known or hereafter invented, without written permission from the publisher.

Published by Next Learning Solutions Press
www.nextlearningsolutionspress.com

ISBN (paperback): 978-1-7357462-0-3
ISBN (ebook): 978-1-7357462-1-0

Edited by David Aretha
Cover and interior design by Christy Collins, Constellation Book Services

Printed in the United States of America

DEDICATION

To the potential of each child
and the leader in all of us

Contents

Foreword   xiii
Preface   xv

INTRODUCTION   1
    Adult learning in the time of COVID   1
    Past Actions   2
    Collaboration Works   3
    A Knowing Gap   4
    Why the Principal?   6
    Principal Preparation   7
    What You'll Find in This Book   8
    Conclusion   8

LET'S PUT THE C IN PLC: AN OVERVIEW   11

CHAPTER ONE: CHARISMATIC LEADERSHIP ≠ SUCCESS   15
    Developing Capacity   16
    Charisma ≠ Success   16
    Charisma = Antithesis of Success   17
    Relationships, Relationships, Relationships   18
    Remote Learning Applications   27
    Wanting More?   27
    Self-Assess and Apply Your Knowledge   29

CHAPTER TWO: TEAM STAFF   31
    The Status Quo   32
    The Alternative: Teaming Teachers   34
    What It Takes: Effective Teams   35
    Summary   45
    Remote Learning Applications   45
    Teacher Teams in Practice   46

Wanting More?	49
Self-Assess and Apply Your Knowledge	50

Chapter Three: Staff Meetings — 51
Focus on Learning	51
Remote Learning Applications	55
Staff Meetings in Practice	55
Self-Assess and Apply Your Knowledge	56

Chapter Four: Principles of Adult Learning — 57
Teachers Teaching Teachers	57
Job-embedded Professional Learning	60
Educators: The Ultimate Knowledge Worker	61
Professional Learning Designs	63
Remote Learning Applications	64
Principles of Adult Learning in Practice	65
Wanting More?	67
Self-Assess and Apply Your Knowledge	68

Chapter Five: Continuous Improvement and Innovation — 69
Leadership = Learning	70
Less Is More: A Few Goals Based on Data	70
Good Goals vs. Bad Goals	72
A Few Goals: Now What?	73
Simple Improvement	77
Innovativeness	79
Sit 'n' Git vs. Git 'r' Done	80
Continuous Improvement and Innovation in Practice (including Remotely)	80
Wanting More?	89
Self-Assess and Apply Your Knowledge	92

Chapter Six: Model Learning — 93
Default Mode: Learning	93
Leadership vs. Management	94

Modeling Professional Learning in Practice (including Remotely)	95
Wanting More?	97
Self-Assess and Apply Your Knowledge	98

Chapter Seven: Allocate Resources — 99

Necessary Resources	100
Specific Resources	101
Allocating Resources in Practice (including Remotely)	107
Self-Assess and Apply Your Knowledge	110

Chapter Eight: Involve Staff — 111

Building Leadership Capacity	112
Leadership ≠ Leader	113
Potential and Right of Leadership	114
Leadership: A Shared Endeavor Requiring Power and Authority Redistribution	115
Input	115
A Plan for Staff Involvement	116
Selecting the Right Work	117
Models of Implementation	118
Staff Involvement in Practice (including Remotely)	120
Wanting More?	122
Self-Assess and Apply Your Knowledge	124

Chapter Nine: Principles of Student Learning — 125

Curriculum	127
Instruction	134
Assessment	139
CIA Summary	147
Wanting More?	148
Self-Assess and Apply Your Knowledge	149

Chapter Ten: Principles of Change and Sustainability — 153

Lead Change—Not Manage Change	154
Relationships, Relationships, Relationships	156

Sustainability	157
Summary of Change	160
Wanting More?	161
Self-Assess and Apply Your Knowledge	162

Chapter Eleven: A Call to Action — 163

Bibliography — *165*
Glossary — *171*
Acknowledgments — *175*

Foreword

There are only two ways to improve your school: 1) Hire better teachers, or 2) Improve the teachers that you have. Outstanding principals know that their primary role with existing staff is to teach the teachers so that they can improve. Creating an environment where collaboration is plentiful is an effective way to do this. Unfortunately, it's not as easy to do as it sounds.

Let's Put the C in PLC recognizes that principals are the filter for the day-to-day reality of your school. By addressing the knowing gap, Dr. Dumas has pulled together research, practices, stories, and tools to help you make your school one where teachers work together to get better. Beginning with your role as a collaborative leader, he provides specific strategies to help you build, develop, and keep positive relationships. Because we know that improvement is always about *people* and never about *programs*, he shares and explains real-world tools for developing the teachers in your school.

Principals who take Chad's work and put it into practice will see high levels of teacher improvement and help the best teachers become even better. They will use small groups to improve instruction and leverage faculty meetings as learning meetings; they will encourage and support staff learning in pursuit of collaborative teamwork. They will prioritize their own learning as a model for the rest of the staff. They will be sure that resources are focused on goals, and have structures to seek input in advance of decisions while gaining feedback after the fact. And they will ignore minor errors in favor of the bigger picture as they ensure high quality curriculum, instruction, and assessment practices in the long, hard work of implementing change.

As an effective principal, you no doubt view yourself as responsible for all aspects of your school. *Let's Put the C in PLC* clarifies the knowledge that you need to make collaboration work for teachers and students, but it is up to you to *make* it happen. As you study this practical guide, be sure to put into practice what you are learning. What distinguishes truly great principals from their counterparts is that they *do* differently. Don't just have an impact, make a difference.

–Todd Whitaker, professor and author of 50 books

Preface

Research demonstrates that a collaborative environment for teachers is critical to improve student learning. The concept of PLCs, or Professional Learning Communities, has been around a while. Unfortunately, due to a variety of factors, there is very little meaningful collaboration that improves educator effectiveness and results for students in most schools. There are misconceptions, false starts, and failed implementation all across the country and world. Full implementation of PLCs is still a long way away. What's a principal to do?

Not only do we know that the most effective way to improve student learning is through creating a collaborative community of adult learners, we also know how important the principal is in creating this PLC. The principal creates the expectations, structures, systems, processes, and space for this work to occur. What's a principal to do?

Finally, we know that there is a gap between knowledge and practice, or a "knowing-doing gap," that plagues just about every aspect of human life—from diet to exercise, from spending to saving, from marital relationships to child-rearing techniques. As an example, I know that I should avoid that morning donut and exercise 30 minutes a day, but I don't do it. I know, but I don't do; hence, I have a knowing-doing gap. And the troubles of the knowing-doing gap make their way into our schools, too. So what's a principal to do?

> Professional learning community works.
> Principals are the key to making it happen.
> Is there a knowing-doing gap?

I was explaining this line of thinking to my wife on a road trip, and she kept asking the same question: So how do you know that principals know what to do?

My response, repeatedly, was, "Of course they know! They're building principals, and they've had experience and an advanced degree to give them this knowledge."

But she persisted: "How do you know that they know?"

And eventually I came to the a-ha moment upon which this work is based: The more important question isn't "What's a principal to do?" Rather, we first need to ask, "What's a principal to know?" First we must be clear about what a principal must **know** in creating a collaborative community of professional learning before seeking to close any potential knowing-doing gap. In other words, first close the knowing gap. As Maya Angelou informally put it, when people know better, they do better.

> "When people know better, they do better."
> —*Maya Angelou*

I combed journal articles, studies, and professional literature in order to identify what principals must know in order to create a culture of collaboration. You may not be surprised with what I found: there was no single compiled list.

Until now.

The result of that study from my award-winning dissertation was a list of 10 elements of principal knowledge. These are key elements that every principal must know in order to create a collaborative community of professional learning for teachers: elements around which this book is focused. The 10 elements are what are needed for a principal to put the "C," a collaborative community, in PLC.

In a nutshell, the 10 Elements of Principal Knowledge (Dumas, 2010) for creating a collaborative workplace environment for teachers are:

1. Recognize that charismatic leadership does not equal success.
2. Team teachers for effectiveness.
3. Focus staff meetings on student learning.
4. Use principles of adult learning.
5. Apply elements of continuous improvement and innovation.
6. Model your own professional learning.
7. Allocate resources.
8. Involve staff in important decisions.
9. Understand principles of student learning.
10. Utilize principles of change and sustainability.

So what is holding us back? Is there a Knowing-Doing Gap with leadership, and specifically principals? Do principals and leaders **know** how to create a collaborative community, the "C," in PLCs with teachers, but simply do not **do** it? Unless we clearly understand what must be **known**, we can never articulate what must be **done**—or bridge a potential Knowing-Doing Gap.

In the end, we all know, knowledge is not enough. "The difference between more effective principals and their less effective colleagues is not what they know. It is what they do" (Whitaker, 2003, p. 1). We must ultimately bridge the knowing-doing gap by putting into practice our understandings, and this is best accomplished by doing. As you learn, try out your new understandings and you will grow through that experience. Learn by doing.

But first things first—develop the knowledge, then apply in practice.

Introduction

Gaps in student performance continue to persist. Millions of students are being left behind, and those who tend to be marginalized—students of color, LGBTQ+ students, English learners, and those from poverty—suffer the most. Both academically and with disciplinary practices, the (at best) inequitable treatment and (at worst) mistreatment of many of these students continues unabated, day by day, week after week, month after month, year after year. And this was pre-COVID.

Then the spring of 2020 happened. Not only did school closures draw our attention to inequities, but the senseless killing of George Floyd, yet another unarmed black man, captured our hearts and led to nationwide protests. While some may have previously been able to bury their heads in the sand, there is now no more excuse. The disparities have become magnified, and our attention, which should have been focused on these inequities for some time, is finally captured. Schools and society have finally started to at least think about, and try to address, the inequities at hand.

Top-down approaches not only won't work, Jim Knight goes even further to state that the top-down model of leadership often *guarantees failure* in professional organizations and communities. This has been tried, and each time it fails. What is needed is a change of heart, a change of culture, and with it, changes in practice. We need to create communities where learning for *all* thrives. Learning for students. Learning for staff. Learning for administrators.

Adult learning in the time of COVID: More important than ever

There has always been a need for adult learning in schools. Indeed, when the learning curve for adults is steep, as it should be, levels of student learning will also be strong. Today the urgency for this professional learning has now been amplified. And the need to work together to meet these needs is even more critical. Put another way, collaborative professional learning, if it was a luxury in the past, is now a necessity.

Physical school closures from the virus, with the resultant challenges of building relationships and engaging students in content, brings with it the need for us to learn about how to build these relationships and engage students in content through remote learning channels. These challenges are both technical and adaptive: one regarding the how-tos of using technology tools, and the other in the actual doing of this work in meeting the needs of kids.

In terms of new technical tools, we have had to learn new ways of engaging students in meaningful learning. Whether using Zoom and breakout rooms, or Google Classroom, or Flipgrid and other video tools, the technology available to us is seemingly endless. Many of us don't even know what these tools are, let alone how to use them. Some of us do know these tools, and some are experts. The need for us to learn from each other has never been more urgent.

While most teachers are masters at building relationships and engaging students in meaningful learning in face-to-face situations, doing this through a screen is far more complex. Who does it well? Who struggles? What tools are they using? How can we learn from their expertise, and how can we continue to refine our practice in mastering these tools? If we ever previously doubted the importance of building a collaborative environment, the intense needs of the day in which we live erases any lingering doubts: COVID has laid bare the need for collaborative adult learning like never before.

Past Actions

In past reform efforts, schools were closed, districts faced reorganization, principals lost their jobs, teachers found other careers, and parents were left searching for successful schools. These are the realities that have come from our persistent failures to meet each child's needs and with increased top-down accountability from the No Child Left Behind Act and subsequent Every Student Succeeds Act.

So what have some of these worst-case "re-structuring" scenarios looked like? Numerous schools saw all of their teaching staff fired. Every single teacher.

Some were hired back. Most weren't. That's because the principal, too, was fired.

It's possible that some of those teachers may have **needed** to be fired long ago. I have no doubt about that. I have worked with more than one teacher who should have moved on to another career.

But my experience throughout the country and world in working with teachers from all segments of society is that the vast majority of teachers are good, caring, loving people who work hard each and every day for their students. They don't come to work every day to be adequate, as implied by "Adequate Yearly Progress" (AYP). They come to work to make a very real difference in the lives of young people, in the next generation, in the future of society. Their hearts are in the right place, even if the culture of the school isn't working to improve their practice.

As alluded to earlier, many of the schools forced into "re-structuring" have been schools with students who have high needs and have been traditionally underserved and marginalized—low income, lacking proper health care, from single-parent families, or with two parents working low-wage jobs who are exhausted when they make it home with little energy to share with their children. These are kids who **need** caring and loving adult relationships. They are kids who **need** stability in their lives because of the lack of stability at home and on the streets. They are kids who **need** a stable school environment, because this is the only stability in their lives.

Yet, federal, top-down legislation disregards these needs when a school fails to meet certain arbitrary accountability measures. These are colossal consequences that we must avert.

Collaboration Works

First of all, let's be very clear: There is no silver bullet; no single answer to school improvement.

But, there *is* a solid track record of decades of experiences of improving student learning by creating a collaborative workplace environment for teachers—creating true Professional Learning Communities. This track record creates a compelling need to look at what must happen in order to create that collaborative culture, and thus avoid the restructuring described above and, worse, failing to meet the needs of our time. The role of the principal, their knowledge and skills, is fundamental to implementing what works.

There may be other paths to successful schools—the restructuring called for by the federal government enunciated above may be one of those. However, if those aren't working for you, this path will. And this path will work *for the long term*, though it also requires a **commitment** for the long term.

Creating a collaborative community will be fun. It will be energizing. It will build momentum and improve student learning. Teachers will come to you and tell you, "I haven't had this much fun teaching in years—maybe ever!" It will be rewarding, and the difference will also show in increased student learning.

Creating a collaborative community of professional learning is also a lot of work. It is not easy, just as nothing worthwhile is ever easy. It will require a reorganization of how you do business. It will require a reorientation toward how you interact with staff. It will require a refocusing on how you make decisions. It will be hard work. Let's do this!

A Knowing Gap

The literature confirms that collaboration—known in many circles as Professional Learning Communities—is an effective strategy for improving student learning and creating successful schools. But collaboration that improves educator effectiveness and results for students is not happening in many schools and districts across this country. Our gaps persist, inequity continues, and our most vulnerable students continue to suffer.

Not only is the role of the principal critical in creating a collaborative environment, as "all change flows through the principal's office" (Murphy, Smylie, Mayrowetz, & Louis, 2009, p. 181), but there is certain fundamental knowledge and skills that principals must possess and do in order to create that collaborative workplace for teachers.

But what if the problem of failure to implement PLCs—or collaborative cultures—was not a *knowing-doing* problem? What if the problem was a *knowing* problem? In the case of a Knowing-Doing Gap, one assumes that knowledge already exists; but what if it doesn't already exist? Knowledge is required for doing, and the knowing-doing gap phenomenon focuses on a problem in *doing* what is already *known*.

What I'm suggesting is that we have a knowing gap. We must first look at the *knowledge* that is required to create this culture, and then fill the gap(s) that principals have. Filling these gaps in *knowledge* will help put the C—a collaborative community—into PLCs.

As an example, Chapter 1 will highlight the importance of building relationships with staff—that many people think leaders must be charismatic. But this is not the case. The research shows that, in many cases, charismatic leadership is associated with *negative* long-term impact. What is needed, instead, is for principals to build relationships.

One key aspect of building relationships is to know the staff. Do principals know that they must know their staff?

At the foundation of each of us is our humanity, and nothing is more important to us than being called by our name. As simple as it sounds, and as much of a no-brainer as it might seem to some, I think it's important to emphasize the need to know the names of your staff. To illustrate the importance of this, let me share a story.

In the third month during their first year as principal at a school, the building principal was conducting a full-length classroom observation as part of the evaluation system for that district. During the lesson, there was an opportunity for the principal to address the teacher in front of the class. The building principal referred to Ms. Smith as Ms. Davis, without recognizing that they called Ms. Smith the wrong name. A student pointed out to the principal that they were mistaken, and the principal replied along these lines, "Ms. Smith, Ms. Davis—same difference."

The principal may have been covering for a simple mistake. I would contend that a truly great leader would, in the spirit of humility, unabashedly proclaim themselves incorrect and apologize instantly—not just in front of the class, but with the teacher individually and possibly even with a handwritten note. Regardless, other situations in the school led staff to believe that the principal really did not know their names—and remember, this was nine weeks into the school year. Needless to say, this failure of the principal undermined their ability to lead. Several years into their tenure, staff still have very little respect for the principal, and positive movement—especially in terms of creating a collaborative workplace environment for teachers—is nonexistent. And, unfortunately, student learning has and likely will continue to suffer.

So what's the point of this story? The principal does not know how important it is to build positive relationships with their staff, and this involves knowing people's names. They don't know that without positive relationships, a collaborative culture cannot exist. A true PLC is not possible—the "C" cannot exist without knowing the staff. And the principal doesn't know that the most powerful route to long-term success of student performance is in creating a collaborative workplace environment for teachers. They likely have a knowing problem—a problem that can be addressed through the implementation of ideas from Chapter One.

Why the Principal?

In a meta-analysis of thousands of studies involving tens of thousands of teachers and hundreds of thousands of learners, researchers Marzano, Pickering, and Pollock (2001) at the Mid-continent Research for Education and Learning (McREL) identified the single most important factor affecting student achievement: ***the quality of the teacher*** and the instructional strategies that they use.

A few years later, Marzano, in cooperation with other researchers at McREL, went on to complete a meta-analysis of the most important factors affecting the quality of the teacher, not to mention the excellence of the school as an organization. Their finding: the most important factor affecting the teacher and the learning process in a school is ***the designated leadership*** within the school (Marzano, Waters, & McNulty, 2005).

Given these two findings, that the teacher has the greatest impact on student learning and that the principal has the greatest impact on the teacher, the development of those in positions of designated leadership, namely principals, is a key place for improving student learning.

Principal Preparation

Prior to someone serving as the principal of a school, one must build knowledge in a wide range of areas. In many states, this includes the completion of certain courses at a master's degree level. As you may already know, classes range from school finance to curriculum design, from philosophy to psychology, from theory to practice. These courses, coupled with, preferably, a couple of years of experience in the education system, are assumed to adequately prepare a person for competence in the role of principal.

Those who have or are serving as a building principal know that this preparation is not enough to be ready for the first day as a principal. The combination of excitement, trepidation, and idealism may not be enough to keep from falling flat on one's face.

The job is overwhelming—managing staff, disciplining students, organizing a master schedule, communicating with parents, dealing with Health and Human Services, partnering with law enforcement—these are just a small handful of the many, many jobs that hit the principal on Day One. On top of all of this, you must meet AYP-like targets and ensure continuous improvement.

In my experience, none of those required courses or experiences provided the basic know-how of creating a collaborative culture. None of the training in the day-to-day experiences of educators prior to walking in that first day was enough.

While collaboration is essential to school improvement, implementation of a collaborative culture just isn't happening around the country. The principal is central to the improvement of student learning, and there is certain knowledge that they must possess in order to create that collaborative workplace environment. This book provides the knowledge principals must have in order to create a culture of collaboration—a collaborative Community of Professional Learning—and thereby improve student learning.

What You'll Find in This Book

Each chapter focuses on one of the ten elements of principal knowledge. The chapter includes a discussion of the key characteristics of that element, as well as a citation of sources that you may want to delve into for further study. Many chapters also have a section devoted to what the element looks like in practice in a building, and applications and tools during a time of remote learning. Finally, there is a short self-assessment to reflect on your own knowledge of that element and to think about bridging any Knowing-Doing Gap that you might have. Of course, the importance of action cannot be overstated. As you know, do. As you do, you will gain insights. And the cycle continues.

My hope is that this book becomes a go-to resource for you. Just like student learning is never a one-and-done proposition, so too must your learning as a professional be reinforced and practiced. This book will lay a foundation for you on the most essential elements that you need to know in order for you to be able to create a collaborative culture for teachers. I hope it becomes well-worn, used in book studies and private contemplation, and in planning and facilitating learning for colleagues and staff.

Conclusion

Unfortunately, as Michael Fullan (2006, p. 14) puts it, Professional Learning Communities may "go the way of just another innovation that captures the limelight ephemerally." This is because there is a foundational lack of understanding of what the concept of PLCs are about—not just a release day here or there, or grouping teachers together for this or that. Rather, PLCs are about a culture: creating a collaborative community of professional learning. What is missing in PLCs is the C—the collaborative community aspect of professional learning.

The professional organization most directly involved with and providing leadership for professional learning, Learning Forward, states that the greatest impact on student learning occurs as a result of the daily collaboration between and amongst staff. Further, the creation of a collaborative culture is "the single most important factor" and "first order of business" (Eastwood & Lewis, 1992, p. 215) for any principal wanting to improve their school. In order to go about making this happen, the principal must know what to do.

So, "what's a principal to know?" Let's start putting the "C" into PLCs.

Let's Put the C in PLC
An Overview

To build a collaborative culture of professional learning, principals need to know and understand these important principles.

1. **Charismatic leadership is not necessary for long-term success**
    A. Relationships ARE necessary for long-term success
    B. Personal Clarity
    C. Dialogue
    D. Rapport
    E. Pause
    F. Paraphrase
    G. Prompt

2. **Teachers should work in teams. Effective elements include:**
    A. Effective grouping
    B. A focus on improving instruction/teaching each other by:
        1. Working, planning, and thinking together
        2. Reflecting via dialogue re: professional issues
        3. Observing and reacting to teaching, curriculum, and assessment
        4. Joint lesson planning and curriculum development
    C. The use of protocols
    D. The training of teachers in the skills and knowledge to collaborate
    E. An incentive system
    F. The deprivatization of the classroom
    G. Networking with teachers in other buildings

3. **Staff meetings should focus on learning and improvement**
    A. Reduce or remove "adminis-trivia" from staff meetings
    B. Lambert's Tenets of Leadership

4. **Principles of adult learning**
    A. External trainings are of limited usefulness because the challenge is to implement what is already known
    B. Characteristics of a Knowledge Worker
        1. Autonomy, complexity, and a connection between effort and reward
    C. Professional learning designs
        1. Assessment as professional learning
        2. Curriculum as professional learning
        3. Data analysis
        4. Lesson study
        5. Instructional coaching
        6. Professional learning communities
        7. Visual dialogue
    D. Job-embedded professional learning

5. **Continuous improvement is necessary. Effective elements include:**
    A. Focusing resources on a small number of goals
    B. Data collection and analysis
    C. The use of multiple sources to guide and demonstrate improvement
    D. Research-based decision-making
    E. A simple focus on refining processes in small ways
    F. Clear, frequent talk about instruction
    G. Recognition and celebration for superior practices and results
    H. Inventiveness/innovativeness where risk-taking is encouraged
    I. High expectations for learning
    J. Using groups as the main units for improvement

6. **Model professional learning by participating in administrator learning communities**
    A. Default mode: Learning
    B. Leadership vs. Management
7. **Resources should be allocated to improve student learning**
    A. Tangible resources
        1. Time
        2. Materials
        3. Equipment
        4. Space
    B. Intangible resources
        1. Training on protocols and procedures
        2. Administrative support
        3. Trust between teachers
        4. Access to new ideas and expertise
8. **Staff should be involved in important decisions**
    A. The use of a leadership team
    B. Opportunity for input is provided, encouraged, expected, implemented
9. **Aspects of student learning**
    A. Curriculum
        1. What students should learn
        2. Alignment of daily objectives with grade-level outcomes to program goals
        3. A variety of Bloom's taxonomy verbs
        4. A variety of Kinds of Targets (KRiSP)
    B. Instruction
        1. Content and Pacing
            a) Daily lessons match curricular expectations
            b) Appropriate instructional level
            c) Pacing appropriate to maintain engagement
        2. Climate

a) Appropriate discipline for orderly environment
b) High expectations
c) Efficient allocation of time
d) Students on task and participating actively
e) Structure for daily routines
f) Many instructional strategies/tools
g) Instructional strategies/tools matched to learning target(s)

C. Assessment
1. Students' involved in assessment process
2. Alignment between EWATR (Expectations, Written curriculum, Assessments, Taught curriculum, and what is Reported)
3. Type of Evidence matches Kind of Target
   a) Teacher Observation: Knowledge, Reasoning, or Skill-level targets
   b) Selected Response: Knowledge-level targets
   c) Extended Written Response: Knowledge, Reasoning, or Product-level targets
   d) Performance Tasks: Reasoning, Skill, and Product-level targets

10. Principles of change and sustainability
   A. Principles of sustainability
   B. Consensus should be built
   C. Persistence is needed
   D. Meaningful change is extremely hard
   E. There is a difference between adaptive and technical barriers

CHAPTER ONE

Charismatic Leadership ≠ Success

Elements of Principal Knowledge in Creating a Collaborative Workplace Environment for Teachers

To build a collaborative culture of professional learning, principals know and understand that:

1. Charismatic leadership is not necessary for long-term success
    A. Relationships ARE necessary for long-term success
    B. Personal Clarity
    C. Dialogue
    D. Rapport
    E. Pause
    F. Paraphrase
    G. Prompt

If you are not a charismatic leader, you're in luck! It turns out that charisma can actually harm long-term success. Nonetheless, if you have charisma, no worries—you can still use your skills and talents in winning people over. Just be aware of the limits of your charisma in terms of long-term success.

The paradigm of leadership, defined as an individual person confirmed with all decision-making abilities, is no more. Leadership of the masses is the new norm, where all individuals have the right and responsibility to serve in leadership roles. This will be discussed more in Chapter Eight. For now, let's focus on you.

Developing Capacity

For the purposes of this book, as the designated leader, your primary responsibility needs to be on developing leadership of others within the organization. Sometimes this is referred to as distributed leadership, shared instructional leadership, building capacity for leadership, balanced leadership, organizational leadership, or principal as professional developer. Whatever you call it, the principal's focus, while it once might have been as an omniscient manager directing folks, is now on building the capacity of all staff in the school.

A symbol of the shift from principal as omniscient manager to that of a builder of capacity can be seen as far back as the federal No Child Left Behind Act of 2001. This law required "that teachers' development be sustained through intensive training embedded in classroom practice and that teachers and administrators develop, as well as evaluate" (Mullen & Hutinger, 2008, p. 279). Developing capacity is part and parcel of leadership.

Charisma ≠ Success

The notion that a charismatic leader can come into a school and save the day, so to speak, is not what schools need (Gronn, 1996). Principals who understand the importance of and need for collaboration, and who work to effectively implement the tenets of a collaborative environment, are more successful in the long run. Improving schools is about working together for success, not about individuals performing miracles. Charismatic leadership is not necessary for success.

A synthesis of this so-called shared endeavor comes from the business world (Kouzes and Posner, 1996, p. 106):

> Leadership is not a solo act. In the thousands of personal-best leadership cases we studied, we have yet to encounter a single example of extraordinary achievement that occurred without the active involvement and support of many people. Fostering collaboration is the route to high performance.

To paraphrase, "school leadership is a team sport" (Fullan, 2003, p. 24).

Charisma = Antithesis of Success

In another business example, Collins (2001) stated that charismatic leaders do not create successful organizations. Instead, it is leaders with a combination of profound humility and intense professional will that lead to lasting greatness. They are unassuming leaders who develop others, create shared commitments, and mobilize the collective energies of the staff—also known as a collaborative environment.

Please don't confuse this Element of Principal Knowledge by subjugating the role of the principal. As noted in the introduction, research on principals can be summarized in the following statement by Murphy et al. (2009): "At the school level all change flows through the principal's office" (p. 181). The principal is absolutely critical to putting the community, a collaborative "C," into PLC.

Let's break down these ideas of profound personal humility and intense professional will into more specific actions. The leaders I have worked with who demonstrate profound personal humility have an overwhelming sense of service for others. They don't allow themselves to be run over by other people, but they do insist that their voice is simply one voice among many. Their voice may be one of greater knowledge, and definitely of a broader perspective in the school, but they do not flaunt their knowledge, perspective, or position in order to get what they want. In fact, they are frequently the last person to express their opinion on any given topic.

Great leaders understand that their role, and the responsibilities associated with it, requires some unilateral decisions. However, they never seek ways to demean, belittle, or even unintentionally reduce the importance of the work of others. They are profoundly humble.

Leaders who demonstrate intense professional will work their tails off. They many times work more hours, and more efficiently within those hours, than any other member of their team. They are dedicated to ongoing learning, and to maximizing their own personal and professional effectiveness. They are about the organization being the absolute best in its field, and about them taking personal responsibility for making sure it happens. With this, too, comes great personal integrity: they walk their talk.

Some may say that these two characteristics of profound humility and intense professional will are dichotomous and therefore impossible to do simultaneously. Yet it is the unique combination of these stellar characteristics that differentiate truly great leaders from the rest. Great leaders find ways to be both humble and driven at the same time.

You may be familiar with a school that had a charismatic leader. You probably experienced the reality that this individual drove significant changes. And they may have even been good changes for kids. But shortly after that person left—and they always do—the significant changes were reversed. That is because long-term success is not associated with charismatic leadership.

So if you have been a charismatic leader, all is not lost. You want your school to succeed. You picked up this book for a reason. Former President George W. Bush stated at one point that, "All childrens [sic] DO learn." I would add, "All principals DO learn."

Relationships, Relationships, Relationships

If charismatic leadership is not necessary for long-term success, what is? As Michael Fullan (2003) succinctly puts it: Relationships, Relationships, Relationships. Positive relationships are the cornerstone of school improvement and the fundamental foundation of building a collaborative culture of professional learning for teachers.

Dennis Sparks, emeritus executive director of Learning Forward, details specific actions that leaders can take to effectively build relationships with staff. Among the most notable are the development of personal clarity and engaging in genuine dialogue. Further, Costa and Garmston elaborate on effective strategies for building relationships through mediating the thinking of others.

Prior to digging into some meaningful discussion around relationships, let me remind you of one very simple strategy that is a must in developing relationships: Know their names.

You can refer back to the story in the introduction about the importance of knowing the names of staff. This was the story of the building principal who could not remember the name of a teacher being observed as part of the formal evaluation. Shockingly, the principal referred to Ms. Smith as Ms. Davis—and failed to recognize her mistake, brushing off the error by noting that the two teachers were effectively one and the same. Needless to say, staff at the building do not trust or respect this principal, and success is limited.

CLARITY

Returning to Dennis Sparks' notion of personal clarity to develop relationships: Deep and meaningful relationships are based upon personal clarity about who you are, where you are going, and how you will get there. Consider even casual relationships around such things as sports. Friends might get together weekly to watch their favorite sports team, unless there's a pandemic, of course. They are clear about who they support, the language they use to support their team, the end goal for the season, etc. If they were not clear about the language, goals, and actions, the relationships would either wither or find another venue where language, goals, and actions *were* clear.

So let's begin with the notion of language as it relates to choice. At the root of personal clarity is a recognition that we all have an element of choice in any given situation. By recognizing this reality and then acting in conformity with it, we send a clear message to others that our vision is clear and our purpose unmistakable. As such, we don't leave folks questioning where we're coming from or wondering what direction we'll take. Instead, if we are clear about our intentions, then others will be clear about our intentions.

One specific strategy a person can use to clarify intentions is to choose your language. A shift in language can signal a shift in mindset that leads to increased clarity in the intentions you have about your personal and professional ambitions. Specifically, shift from using phrases like "I have to…" to instead saying "I choose to…" or, "I am going to…."

Instead of saying, "I have to clean the house this weekend," you might say, "I'm going to clean the house this weekend." This is because you like a clean house.

Or "I choose to complete the report due to the state by Friday." This is because it makes you feel better knowing that it's done. Or "I choose to spend time in the office completing paperwork instead of being in classrooms." This is because it might be what you are used to doing, or because it feels good to get the paperwork done. Or "I choose to spend staff meetings focused on managerial issues." This might be because this is the stuff that staff has always talked about, and if it's not part of the meetings you'll have a revolt on your hands.

Instead of "having" to engage in certain activities, a person "chooses" to engage in those activities. After all, at the heart of every endeavor, we fundamentally do have a choice, as difficult or hidden as that choice might be, or even when you feel like there is no real choice. Clarifying the language that we use to signal that we are choosing one activity over another activity not only clarifies for ourselves, but also displays to others our true intentions.

A second strategy you can pursue to gain greater personal clarity is through the development of stretch goals, followed by plans of action with many ways to achieve these goals. Sparks emphasizes the importance of "stretch goals" being such that, when we set them, by definition, we don't think that we can reach them. The process of developing a stretch goal clarifies what we really want, and focuses our intentions on that goal.

Once stretch goals are initiated, it is important to identify many paths to achieving those goals. Identifying only one or two paths to the achievement of your goals stymies creativity and, ultimately, the attainment of the goal. I like what Sparks (2007, p. 17) says, that "getting a good idea begins with getting your hands on many ideas." The first plan you develop for achieving your goal will likely not be that "good idea," so the development of many paths is critical to gaining clarity about what your stretch goal really is, what it entails, and how you will get there.

Finding many paths can take many ways. Maybe you research online, or you contact an institution of higher education, or you consult with your district office, or you engage in dialogue with your School Improvement Team, or you use any number of these (and other) strategies.

> Relationships are founded upon clarity
> of language, goals, and actions.

One more point: great leaders who are clear about their intentions write. Good writing is good thinking, and good thinking is good writing. It doesn't have to be major dissertations on subjects, but rather could be simple "chicken scratches" on edges of notepaper, comments in your calendar, or other short writings. The process of writing your thinking down creates clarity of intention, whether in language, goals, or actions.

DIALOGUE

Paulo Freire (1970) provides the most beautiful of definitions for dialogue, coupled with the conditions necessary to make it happen. According to Freire, dialogue is "an act of creation" and that "without dialogue there is no communication, and without communication, there can be no true education." He elucidates by identifying six principles, or pre-conditions, for dialogue to occur: love, humility, faith, trust, hope, and critical thinking. Because his commentary is succinct, I will simply quote his work and encourage you to think deeply about what each of these principles mean for you and your interactions.

Love

"Dialogue cannot exist, however, in the absence of a profound love for the world and for people.... Love is at the same time the foundation of dialogue and dialogue itself.... Because love is an act of courage, not of fear, love is commitment to others.... If I do not love the world—if I do not love life—if I do not love people—I cannot enter into dialogue."

Humility

"[D]ialogue cannot exist without humility.... Dialogue, as the encounter of those addressed to the common task of learning and acting, is broken if the parties (or one of them) lack humility.

"At the point of encounter there are neither utter ignoramuses nor perfect sages; there are only people who are attempting, together, to learn more than they now know."

Faith

"Dialogue further requires an intense faith in humankind, faith in their power to make and remake, to create and re-create, faith in their vocation to be more fully human. Faith in people is an *a priori* requirement (a necessary prerequisite) for dialogue; the "dialogical [person]" believes in others even before he meets them face to face.... Without this faith in people, dialogue is a farce which inevitably degenerates into paternalistic manipulation."

Trust

"Founding itself upon love, humility, and faith, dialogue becomes a horizontal relationship of which mutual trust between the dialoguers is the logical consequence. It would be a contradiction in terms if dialogue—loving, humble, and full of faith—did not produce this climate of mutual trust, which leads the dialoguers into ever closer partnership in the naming of the world.... Whereas faith in humankind is an *a priori* requirement for dialogue, trust is established by dialogue.... False love, false humility, and feeble faith in others cannot create trust. Trust is contingent on the evidence which one party provides the others of his true, concrete intentions; it cannot exist if that party's words do not coincide with their actions. To say one thing and do another—to take one's own word lightly—cannot inspire trust."

Hope

"Nor yet can dialogue exist without hope.... Hopelessness is a form of silence, of denying the world and fleeing from it.... As the encounter of women and men seeking to be more fully human, dialogue cannot be carried on in a climate of hopelessness. If the dialoguers expect nothing to come of their efforts, their encounter will be empty and sterile, bureaucratic and tedious."

Critical Thinking

"Finally, true dialogue cannot exist unless the dialoguers engage in critical thinking—thinking which discerns an indivisible solidarity between the world and the people and admits of no dichotomy between them… which perceives reality as process, as transformation, rather than as a static entity…which does not separate itself from action…"

THREE + ONE

The foundational principles of dialogue enunciated by Freire possess a level of depth and complexity that is beyond the intention of this book. However, I have found that the practical application of these principles can be boiled down into a handful of actions that a person can take to facilitate dialogue: what I call the "3 + 1" moves from Costa and Garmston. These are pause, paraphrase, and prompt, (3) within the context of building rapport (+1). Leaders who are grounded in Freire's principles and who employ these 3 + 1 moves are able to more effectively engage in dialogue, and, thus, build positive relationships with staff that will lead to long-term improvement and success.

The +1, rapport, is the context for our work to create dialogical relationships, and lays a foundation for the three moves that we'll talk about in a bit. Costa and Garmston provide a full and scientific description of rapport—I simply define it as being in relationship with another person. When you are in relationship with another person, and they are in relationship with you, each person is comfortable. This rapport manifests in certain conditions that begin to emerge: one of which is the mirroring of body language—a powerful nonverbal source of communication.

Individuals who are in rapport will have similar body language—if one person uses large arm gestures, the other person will do the same; if one person is leaning back in their chair, the other does the same; if one person is sitting cross-legged, the other person does the same.

The next time you're at a public restaurant, notice the people around you. Notice those who are in rapport and those who are not. Notice, for example, the couple, both leaning into each other with arms up on the table. Notice those who are not in relationship, and you will notice people who are not mirroring each other's body language.

Please note the use of the word "mirror," not "mimic." Individuals who are in rapport with each other are naturally mirroring one another. It's not a gimmick or a game, but a natural outgrowth of being in relationship. Hence, if you want to build rapport with someone, a key place to start is the nonverbal communication method of body language. Notice it. Notice their language and tone. And then strive to quickly get into rapport with them by mirroring their movements.

One way to "test" if you're actually in rapport with someone is to shift your own body—arms, legs, or otherwise—and see if the other individual follows. More than likely, if you're in rapport, the other person will follow your lead within five seconds or so. If you're not in rapport, they won't follow and you need to continue to strive for rapport by mirroring them.

In addition to the nonverbal "plus one" of rapport, there are three specific moves for building relationship with individuals that Costa and Garmston describe: pause, paraphrase, and prompt.

Pausing in dialogue with someone is exactly what it sounds like: pausing. People need time to think and to process. Give them the gift of that space by simply pausing.

> "Listening is only powerful and effective if it is authentic. Authenticity means that you are listening because you are curious and because you care, not just because you are supposed to. The issue, then, is this: Are you curious? Do you care?"
> Stone et al. 1999

As a building principal, people are bombarding you all day long with this problem or that issue. Don't interrupt them. Don't immediately jump in with your solution. Instead, give them space to think—five seconds will usually suffice. When you give people the gift of space to think they will come up with far better solutions than you ever will. Give them the gift of space, of silence. Pause. Take a breath. Then you can encourage them to take action and commend them for their thoughtful solutions.

A second powerful move that you can make is the paraphrase. In my own experience as a school leader, folks come to me with problems. Though we don't typically know at first, many times people simply want to be heard. Nothing more and nothing less. The process of paraphrasing for another person allows them to know that they've been heard and understood. This communicates to them their value as a person, as well as their value as a professional.

When paraphrasing, Costa and Garmston counsel to avoid the term "I," as in "I think I hear you saying." Instead, use stems like, "So you're thinking that…" or "You feel as though…" or "You're seeing this…." This implies that you must be paying careful attention to the speaker so that you can accurately paraphrase. And the paraphrase cannot be contrived or shallow, but, rather, a sincere acknowledgment of the other person's concerns/needs and reflection back. Finally, the paraphrase should not be longer than their statements—it's not about you; it's about them.

One final note about paraphrasing: Don't be surprised if, after you have paraphrased, the speaker then expounds on their thinking. If you have been successful in paraphrasing, they will frequently keep speaking. That means that you must keep listening, and continuing to pause, paraphrase, and prompt. At some point, you will encourage their follow-through, as their solution(s) may seem or be difficult. Remind them that they can do hard things. They do them every day. They, too, work in education!

A final action is that of prompting (or sometimes referred to as posing a question). Used in combination with pausing and paraphrasing, it can be helpful to building relationships.

Again, rather than jumping into a person's thinking, prompt their thinking (typically after engaging in a paraphrase). Pose an open-ended question; or ask for more information on a specific point; or ask for a clarification of key material; or ask for their opinion on how to move forward. The process of prompting will allow the other person to feel valued and heard, to dig deeper into their own thinking. They can talk through what they already know and come to their own conclusion.

Colleagues have shared with me the power of these three moves in my own leadership. Over my career, I have directly supervised a number of principals, teacher leaders, teachers, and administrative assistants. In all of these situations, I typically meet quite regularly to touch base on their work and how I can serve them and their programs.

Inevitably, at pretty much every meeting, there would be some dilemma that they and/or their program or school was experiencing. I purposefully used these moves by allowing them to fully share the issue under consideration. Instead of jumping in with my own thoughts, I would intentionally pause and think—typically moving my eyes away from theirs to signal my thinking (and sometimes accompanied by an intentional movement of my body to also signal this thinking and find out if we were in rapport). Almost every time, they would pick up and start talking more about the issue, further clarifying their own thinking and possible outcomes.

After that initial pause, I regularly paraphrased the issue and/or their thinking around it. The response was either a confirmation that I "had" it, or them expounding further. If they expounded further, another paraphrase may have been called for.

At some point we were on the same proverbial page together, at which time I moved to prompting through the use of a question. More often than not, my question was along the lines of, "Given what you have shared and your expertise in this area, what are your hunches about how we might move forward?" This typically resulted in *them* pausing and then identifying one or more possible solutions to move forward.

What these colleagues have shared with me over the years is that, because of these actions, they felt trusted **by me** and, therefore, had trust **in me**, as well. They contrasted my handling of our meetings with the handling of other colleagues and supervisors and particularly noted how trust was completely absent from those other interactions. In other words, utilizing these skills allowed us to build trust, have rapport, build capacity, and, most importantly, put the "C" in PLC.

Remote Learning Applications

In many ways, the term "social distancing" is inappropriate. What we have needed during the COVID-19 pandemic is not social distancing but physical distancing. Indeed, the importance of relationships and the social aspect of our humanity has never been more pronounced. From singing on balconies in New York and Italy to virtual happy hours, and from visiting our loved ones through windows of healthcare facilities to developing stronger community connections in our neighborhoods, relationships are at the core of what it means to be humans. In many cases we have learned that, because learning is remote, it is even more important to develop relationships with our colleagues and staff.

In a virtual environment, your *intentionality* to build relationships is critical. Do you start meetings with a quick human touch-base? Do you make sure to meet with each staff member each week on a one-on-one level (starting with a chat about how they are doing)? With virtual meetings, wait time needs to almost double what we typically provide—are you providing that space for thinking? In the final analysis, are you *living* Freire's principles of effective dialogue? As I have heard many times over the years regarding students, "They don't care how much you know until they know how much you care." It's true of adults, too.

WANTING MORE?

Sparks, D. (2007). *Leading for Results (2nd ed.).* Thousand Oaks, CA: Corwin.

A few years ago, I went to a two-day seminar with Dennis Sparks at the Annual Learning Forward Conference. It was such an amazing life- and professional-changing experience that I went to the exact same session the following year. He distills incredibly complex subjects into simple "Teachable Points of View" (TPOV), and has amazing clarity about professional learning and leadership.

This particular text of Sparks is built like a workbook. A few pages of thought-provoking text are provided, followed by a series of questions and space for deep thought and application in one's own work. Leading for Results is not to be read like a textbook, but rather over time with great concentration, practice in one's life, and, ideally, reflection with other leaders in similar situations. If there was one text that I would recommend to every leader, it would be this.

Collins, J. (2001). *Good to Great: Why Some Companies Make the Leap…And Others Don't.* New York: HarperCollins.

In a synthesis of 40 years of research from the business world on the most successful organizations, Collins identifies the outperformers as measured by a statistical analysis of comparison against the stock market. In studying the common denominators of those outperformers, he identified "Level 5" leadership as the single most important factor for long-term success. Level 5 leaders possess a unique mixture of intense personal humility and strong professional will and strive to develop the capacity of others in their organization.

Garmston, R. J. and Wellman, B. M. (2016). *The Adaptive School: A Sourcebook for Developing Collaborative Groups.* Lanham, MD: Rowman & Littlefield.

The work of the Thinking Collaborative (www.thinking-collaborative.com) focuses on building identity and capacity as collaborators, inquirers, and leaders. Their resources, tools, and trainings provide a wealth of material from which to cull in order to improve your own practice as a collaborator, inquirer, and leader. The website is quite rich to get you started, and if you want more, the sourcebook is dense and detailed to assist you on your journey. The explanations of rapport, pausing, paraphrasing, and prompting provided here are very brief. I recommend the sourcebook for in-depth descriptions, examples, and tools to develop your own skills and identity. The foundation seminar and advanced seminar are well worth your time, as well, to improve your skills, clarify your own identity, and build a team that puts the "C" in PLC.

Self-Assess and Apply Your Knowledge

Use the following table to self-assess your knowledge on each of the statements. Note how you go about bridging any knowing-doing gap in order to make each one a reality.

	I need to learn more	I know this	I can teach others	What I DO to make this happen
Learning is greatly improved when all teachers are engaged in leadership roles				
Improvement is NOT conditional upon charismatic leadership				
I must be profoundly humble				
I must demonstrate intense professional will				
I must know the names of all the staff				
My language should reflect choice				
I need to set stretch goals				
I need to identify many paths to reaching my goals				
In order to engage in dialogue, I must **love** the people I am serving				
In order to engage in dialogue, I must have **faith** in other people and humankind				
In order to engage in dialogue, I must **trust** others, including alignment between my words and actions				
In order to engage in dialogue, I must have **hope** for a better future and world				
In order to engage in dialogue, I must **think critically** in understanding process and not static reality				
I must mirror body language with those with whom I'm seeking to build relationships				
I must provide space (silence) for others in order to mediate their thinking and build relationships with others				
I must paraphrase conversations to make sure others feel understood, and thus build relationships				
I must ask open-ended questions to build relationships with others				

CHAPTER TWO

Team Staff

Elements of Principal Knowledge in Creating a Collaborative Workplace Environment for Teachers

To build a collaborative culture of professional learning, principals know and understand that:

2. Teachers should work in teams. Effective elements include:
   A. Effective grouping
   B. A focus on improving instruction/teaching each other by:
      1. Working, planning, and thinking together
      2. Reflecting via dialogue re: professional issues
      3. Observing and reacting to teaching, curriculum, and assessment
      4. Joint lesson planning and curriculum development
   C. The use of protocols
   D. The training of teachers in the skills and knowledge to collaborate
   E. An incentive system
   F. The deprivatization of the classroom
   G. Networking with teachers in other buildings

The Ten Elements of Principal Knowledge for Creating a Collaborative Culture are, intentionally, not ranked in terms of order of importance. With this in mind, the first element does seem to build a foundation upon which the others rest—quality relationships for putting the "C" in PLC. If I were to emphasize another one, it would be this second element because of how important it is for teachers to be teamed. And knowing how to make those teams effective is even more important.

"One of the most frequently mentioned resources important to the effective functioning of a school is the professional development opportunities for teachers" (Marzano et al., 2005, p. 59). While this quote is more than a decade old, it still rings true today. But professional development is not and cannot be confined to external trainings—those one-shot workshop wonders with the external expert presenting to an auditorium of teachers. These are of limited usefulness.

Learning Forward emphasizes that "the most powerful forms of staff development occur in ongoing teams that meet on a regular basis…for the purposes of learning, joint lesson planning, and problem solving" (NSDC, 2003, p. 59). Principals must invest in teacher learning by providing time for educators to work, plan, and think together.

To dig into this concept of teacher teaming, this chapter will do three things as part of the summary of what it takes to effectively team teachers. First, we'll take a look at the dangers of keeping the status quo, of leaving the current system in place where teachers are essentially private and independent contractors. Second, we'll take a look at the very real potential of teaming teachers. Finally, we'll examine what it takes to create effective teams in your school. As with other chapters in this book, there will be a case study, a *Wanting More?* section, and a self-reflection tool.

The Status Quo

As a teacher, I had my classroom, my kids, my textbooks. I was regularly at school well before 7:45 a.m. and after 3:15 p.m.—our contracted start and end to the day. Students shuffled into my classroom at regular 49-minute intervals, and I had a planning period somewhere in the middle. Because I was at a middle school, we had a team planning time—so about once a week we met to discuss issues. This usually translated into: Who are the problem kids, and what are the kids going to do to change their behavior?

These professional interactions with my colleagues were by no means bad. We had every good intention in the world to help kids. Outside of the food that someone was assigned to bring once a month, the development of a sense of collaborative community was minimal, at best. And professional learning was nonexistent. While enjoyable, these meetings did not put the "C" in PLC.

My experience is not unlike the vast majority of teachers' experiences. The DuFour's sometimes refer to high schools as a collection of independent contractors connected by a common parking lot. We as educators rarely see each other in professional settings, and we rarely speak with each other using the language of our profession. Sure, we see each other in the parking lot as we arrive and leave school. We are friendly enough—we say hello in the hallway, or even sit together at lunch. But the interactions are superficial. We simply say "hello" and "goodbye." Meaningful professional dialogue, focused on improving student learning, is at a minimum in most schools.

Before examining the potential, realistic, and documented benefits of putting the "C" in PLC, let us consider the reality of continuing the status quo in many schools: continued privatization of classrooms.

Teacher isolation is one of the greatest barriers to improving student learning. The consequences are colossal. Privatization ensures that teachers teach whatever they like and however they like. This means that the basic notion of a guaranteed curriculum for students, parents, and the community becomes null and void. The school board may officially approve a curriculum guide for all subjects and grade levels, yet privatization of classrooms ensures that when the door to the classroom closes, the teacher has all control over what is taught. And in this setting, curriculum guides become, quite literally, well-intended fiction.

A second consequence of this teacher isolation is that it results in minimal monitoring of the quality of teacher work, and ultimately impact (or lack thereof), on student learning. Unless a principal can have super vision (as implied by combining the two terms into one word, "supervision"), it is impossible to effectively monitor the quality of teacher work. And the futility of one-person oversight is glaring when juxtaposed against the need to build the leadership capacity of staff. Chapter Eight will have a full-scale elaboration of this concept.

Finally, teacher isolation creates inequity. Two (or more) teachers teaching the same course may or may not have the same student learning outcomes. Assessments may be quite different. With teacher isolation, student learning, assessing, and grading are variables. As a former assistant secretary of education is fond of saying, "It shouldn't be the luck of the draw that my grandson receives instruction from a qualified teacher" (R. J. Simon, public presentation, April 2004).

If we stay on the current trajectory for student learning, then the quality of curricular, instructional, and assessment practices is largely dependent on random placement of a child in a classroom. If we want to guarantee the curriculum for every child and ensure that high-quality instructional and assessment practices are the norm in every classroom, then the walls of privatization must come down: the deprivatization of practice is essential to improving student learning.

The Alternative: Teaming Teachers

Little calls it collective autonomy, and Darling-Hammond and McLaughlin refer to it as a collective Professional Learning Community. Still others refer to this environment as a collaborative culture. Regardless of the specific title, this 'collective autonomy' will always achieve better results than individuals working under close, rigid supervision" (Schmoker, 2005, p. 146).

Newmann and Wehlage (1995, p. 31) articulate collective autonomy as being teachers who work productively "to participate in reflective dialogue to learn more about professional issues," "observe and react to one another's teaching, curriculum, and assessment practices," and "engage in joint planning and curriculum development." These same researchers go on to summarize this collective autonomy into three key areas of collaboration: "implementing curriculum, instruction, and assessment" (p. 38).

When groups of teachers work together to accomplish these three tasks, the process "facilitate[s] development of shared purposes for student learning and collective responsibility to achieve it" (Newmann

& Wehlage, p. 38). The key phrase, though, is that "groups, rather than individuals, are seen as the main units" (p. 38) for doing this work. The basic elements of curriculum, instruction, and assessment must be done collaboratively with other teachers, and not in isolation, to truly develop collective autonomy and therefore improve student learning.

The word "implementing" implies that teachers are not simply grouped for the sake of grouping. Rather, there are specific actions (i.e., implementation) that are taken to improve teacher practice, and it is the principal who establishes a collaborative working environment for teachers. For example, in schools where a collaborative culture exists, principals don't just encourage collaboration; rather, they create structures and expectations to make sure teachers work together in teams. Even though this systematic collaboration goes against the norm of teacher isolation, teachers ultimately respond positively. When teachers are given time and support for their collaborative work, they say that collaboration is useful, stimulating, and helpful. Providing opportunities for teachers to network outside of their building provides even more momentum for collaboration.

> "The leader's function is to provide opportunities for teachers to work together in self-managing teams to improve *their own* instruction, always with the expectation for improved learning."
> emphasis in original, Schmoker, 2005, p. 147

What It Takes: Effective Teams

Effective collaboration means that teachers:

1. "participate in reflective dialogue to learn more about professional issues,"
2. "observe and react to one another's teaching, curriculum, and assessment practices," and

3. "engage in joint planning and curriculum development" (Newmann & Wehlage, 1995, p. 31).

Effective teams *must* focus on these three areas. Otherwise, the teams of teachers will not be effective.

Learning Forward discussed the focus for effective teacher teams in a little bit different language: "Staff Development that improves the learning of all students…organizes adults into learning communities whose goals are aligned with those of the school and district" (NSDC, 2003, p. 59). Since that time, Learning Forward has further clarified (2011) that "Professional learning that increases educator effectiveness and results for all students occurs within learning communities committed to continuous improvement, collective responsibility, and goal alignment."

Lieberman and McLaughlin (1995) noted the essential nature of collaboration in improving student learning by highlighting that involvement in collaborative activities "encourages exchange among the members [and] assures teachers that their knowledge of their students and of schooling is respected. Once they know this, they become committed to change, willing to take risks, and dedicated to self-improvement" (p. 66).

Two more points, before heading into some specifics around grouping staff and protocols and structures: First, principals must understand and implement an incentive system that ensures collaborative work, and, second, they must provide opportunities for teachers to network outside of their building. Incentive systems do not need to be tangible—simple praise and recognition for growth are some of the most powerful ways to incentivize colleagues. Fun certificates and traveling trophies honoring specific aspects of teamwork are one way that this can happen. And, somewhat connected to incentives, is providing opportunities for teachers to visit teachers in other buildings and districts. Sharing of ideas is important not only *within* the school building, but between school buildings and systems. Covering a teacher's class (yourself) is a great way to do this if substitute teachers are hard to come by.

GROUPING TEACHERS

Simply grouping colleagues for the sake of grouping will not create a collaborative culture. As noted by Fullan (2020), groups can be powerfully wrong. And as DuFour and Berkey (1995) put it: "principals must not mistake congeniality with collegiality." A classroom teacher wouldn't allow "BFFs" (Best Friends Forever) to work together regularly in their classroom; so, too, must you group teachers so as to focus on improving their practice. Congeniality may or may not result, but collegiality must be a priority.

First of all, the ideal number of people on a team is three to five. Two people might get along well (or not), but the flow of ideas can be limited. Six people or more in a group requires more skilled facilitation to elicit the expertise of all members. If you have larger numbers of staff and find yourself with six or more people in a group, the solution is simple: break the group of six into two groups of three.

Grouping of teachers needs to be based on what makes sense—not just to you, but to the team of teachers. This begins by simply talking with teachers to find out what makes sense. One configuration might make sense to you while a completely different one might make sense to them. Together, you can navigate these differences, and at the end of the day the grouping needs to be based on what will improve educator practice and results for students. I can almost guarantee, though, that if you designate groupings in your office with little input from staff (see Chapter Eight for more on involving staff in important decision-making), success will be limited and you will likely have an insignificant impact.

Groupings of teachers can be based on a number of factors, including content area (e.g., Algebra I teachers work together), grade level (third grade teachers), student needs (a middle school team), or any number of other ways. Additionally, these groupings should not be a "one-and-done" proposition. The same groups do not need to meet in perpetuity, or even for an entire year. Maybe they change each unit, quarter, or semester—based on what will increase educator effectiveness and results for students. What is non-negotiable is that all teachers must work in teams if you want to put the "C" into PLC; all staff must be on some team to improve their practice.

One more word about the notion that all staff must be on a team. The importance of collaborating *with* teachers to identify meaningful teams cannot be overstressed. Singletons, in particular, are too often lumped together, or randomly assigned to grade-level or department teams. Don't make this mistake. Meaningful collaboration is needed for all adults, and simply throwing them into groups for your own ease won't work—and will likely create resentment. Treat your specialists as the professionals that they are, and engage them in identifying the most useful structures for them to improve their practice and results for all students.

> **An incredible, detailed listing of dozens and dozens of protocols is available for free online from the School Reform Initiative (https://www.schoolreforminitiative.org/protocols/).**
>
> **Do your own searches online, as well, and you'll find a plethora of excellent protocols for just about any situation.**

PROTOCOLS AND STRUCTURES

Second, protocols and structures need to be in place to ensure that leadership responsibilities rotate between and among staff. As human beings, we need more than simple encouragement for collaboration—we need structures and expectations to facilitate this collaboration. Fortunately, Easton, in partnering with Learning Forward and significant thinkers and practitioners in the field of staff development, identified two dozen designs for powerful professional learning because of their potential for creating a collaborative culture. There are several designs most specifically appropriate for creating a collaborative culture with teams of teachers. Examples of these will be provided later, but to get you started, those seven are:

- Curriculum as professional learning
- Assessment as professional learning
- Data analysis
- Lesson study
- Instructional coaching
- Professional Learning Communities
- Visual dialogue

None of these are one-time activities, nor are they simply behaviors to accomplish. Rather, they are categories of effective designs for professional learning that go beyond traditional "sit 'n' gits," also known as workshops, trainings, or conferences.

Curriculum as Professional Learning

The process of writing down what we expect students to know and be able to do is known as curriculum design. From the analysis of state or national standards to the writing of daily objectives, from the development of District curriculum guides to evaluating textbooks or other resources, from examining gaps in objectives to developing daily lessons—these are a few of the options available to principals who seek to engage staff in curriculum design.

Chapter Nine lays out more details on quality curriculum design work. For now, suffice it to say that curriculum work is never finished. Every time a team meets—whether daily, weekly, or any time between—teachers should be engaged in clarifying what students should know and be able to do. Whether this takes the form of specifically writing down curriculum objectives, or in designing appropriate assessments to inform instruction, or in developing units of study or specific lessons, the work of teams should always come back to curriculum design.

Assessment as Professional Learning

The process of designing quality assessments draws upon a wealth of professional expertise:

- First of all, what do we need to measure?
- Second, what kind of target are we measuring (Knowledge, Reasoning, Skill, or Product)?
- Third, what type of evidence (Selected Response, Extended Written Response, Performance Task, or Teacher Observation), based on the kind of target, will we accept to demonstrate student learning?
- And, finally, what is the specific tool that we will use—rubric, test, checklist, etc?

These are high-level questions that require clarity on the part of the teachers about what they are teaching and, therefore, assessing. And it requires skill to collaborate and actually develop or revise the assessment tool.

For a fuller discussion of assessment as professional learning, see Chapter Nine. In that chapter, you will learn more about quality assessment. For now, understand that high-quality assessment is the responsibility of *every* educator. None of us can shirk this responsibility. Whether teams are formed based on common students or content does not matter—what matters is that every educator is engaged in improving their assessment practice.

Data Analysis

A colleague once stated that schools suffer from "data-rhea:" a condition of having so much data that we don't know what to do with it. The process of data analysis for teacher teams, on the other hand, is a step-by-step look at how our kids are performing. It involves some basic data literacy—like the difference between norm- and criterion-referenced tests, the difference between percent and percentile, the difference between cohort and program data, the differences between perception, program, demographic, and performance data, and others. If you are fuzzy on these differences, then it's time to get familiar with the resource at the end of this chapter, and you can start with the Data Boot Camp Knowledge Map as a brief primer included here.

Data Boot Camp Knowledge Map

School Improvement (SI) Process

1. The school improvement process is best carried out **collaboratively and reflectively**
2. School improvement is focused on **improving the learning of all students**
3. Five questions we ask ourselves in the SI process:
   a. **Where are we now?**
   b. **Where are we going?**
   c. **How will we get there?**
   d. **How will we know that we got there?**
   e. **How will we sustain the effort?**
4. The leadership team should include **administrators, teachers, parents, community members, and students**

Data Terminology

5. The four types of data are **Achievement, Perception, Program, and Demographic**
6. Achievement data tells us **how well students are doing** and includes **Norm-Referenced Tests** (NRTs), Criterion-Referenced Tests (CRTs), **IEP achievement data, report card grades, AP, ACT and SAT scores,** etc.
7. Demographic data tells us **who the students are** and includes **gender, race, ethnicity, socio-economic status (SES), mobility, English Learners, suspension and expulsion rates, special education**, etc.

8. Program data tells us **who the teachers are and what the curriculum is** and includes **instructional program data, professional development data, school organization data, parental involvement data, staff data,** etc.
9. Perception data tells us **how people feel about the school** and includes **surveys, student and staff wellness and absenteeism information, discipline reports, parent/community volunteerism**, etc.
10. The two types of standardized assessments are **Norm-referenced** (NRT or NRA) and **Criterion-referenced** (CRT or CRA)
11. Norm-referenced assessments/tests (NRA/NRTs) are reported in **percentile and compare students to all others taking the test**
12. Criterion-referenced assessments/tests (CRA/CRTs) **assess an individual's performance on a specific set of standards or criteria**
13. **Raw scores, scale scores, percentile rank, and grade equivalents are NOT on equidistant scales** and can NOT be directly compared with each other or other scoring methods

Data Analysis Process

14. Data is used to discover **patterns and relationships**
15. Triangulation of data is using **multiple data sources** to make decisions
16. Data analysis methods include **describing, counting, factoring, clustering, comparing, seeking trends or patterns, examining outliers, finding co-variation, eliminating rival explanations, and modeling**

17. Data can be compared **individually, or in a cohort, panel, or selected comparison group**
18. The steps to analyzing achievement data are **1) study the data, 2) determine expectation levels, 3) create a numeric table, 4) color code the data, 5) create a graphic representation of the numeric table, 6) record observations, 7) record hypotheses**
19. Disaggregating data involves **looking at sub-groups** and might include **skill pattern data leading to individual test item and/or individual student data, demographic data, perception data, and program data**
20. After making hypotheses, the team must conduct research to either **accept or reject** them

Lesson Study

Lesson study is a step-by-step process of co-planning a lesson, then having one teacher deliver the lesson while the other colleagues observe. The process then proceeds to in-depth reflection and analysis on what worked and didn't work. Finally, teams consolidate their learning by developing specific actions for implementation in all of their classrooms based on the learning from the lesson.

While primarily geared toward grade-alike or content-area teams, this method of professional learning also works between subject areas and grade levels. The key is to focus on what students are to learn, co-planning the lesson, and then reflecting on what did and did not work. Individuals critically reflect on the instruction so that all members of the lesson study team improve their practice.

Instructional Coaching

Just as coaches in athletics are guides who provide an objective view of reality followed by specific suggestions for improvement, coaches in education provide the same service (though there are various models that differ in the suggestion arena). Some schools may have the resources to hire a person specifically as a coach, while others may build the capacity of a number of fellow teachers on the staff to serve in this role. Regardless of the approach, the process of coaching staff to get better results can be a powerful tool to improve the effectiveness of teams.

Instructional coaches use a number of ways to engage teachers in professional learning. In one model, the teacher videotapes a lesson and the two sit down together to reflect on the lesson and plan their learning. In another, the coach watches the teacher teach and provides feedback in a non-evaluative way. In yet another, the coach works with a team of teachers to improve their practice. Regardless of the specific method used, the importance of the coach being a partner with the teacher and providing non-evaluative feedback is paramount.

Professional Learning Communities

This entire book is about Professional Learning Communities, and there are some specific structures that can be quite helpful. Whole Faculty Study Groups (WFSGs) (Murphy and Lick, 2005) is one specific approach to developing effective teams. A cycle is used, and staff are grouped in specific ways based on the analysis of data. In other words, teams of teachers are not based on grade level or content area, but on student need.

WFSGs are powerful tools, and by themselves can move your staff a long way toward improving student learning. A specific learning cycle in a study group may last a few weeks or a few months, but rarely a full year. The learning from the study group must be fully focused on the professional practice of the teachers.

Visual Dialogue

Visual dialogue is a process with tools or templates to facilitate the effective functioning of groups. Through the use of these tools, teams will develop a clear understanding of where they want to go in improving their practice that increases student learning. Further, it will assist teams in identifying action steps that they can take. Finally, it will provide a succinct description of what success will look like. For more information and for a detailed look at the tools and processes called for in Visual Dialogue (or these other designs), see Easton's (2015) *Powerful Designs for Professional Learning*.

Summary

Keeping the current state of professionalism in education, that of privatized practice, will not improve student learning. The practice of teachers serving as, essentially, private practitioners only serves to exacerbate student learning gaps. What's more, most teachers yearn (or will learn to yearn!) for opportunities to collaborate.

Teachers need more than simple encouragement—they need structures and expectations to facilitate this collaboration. Principals must invest in teacher learning by providing time for educators to work, plan, and think together. Designs like those mentioned by Easton will increase the effectiveness of teacher teams.

Remote Learning Applications

The considerations for teaming of teachers, together with the professional learning designs discussed in this chapter, are just as important in a virtual environment as in face-to-face settings. If the need for ongoing learning for teachers wasn't evident before the pandemic hit, it has since been placed front and center. From learning new technical tools to figuring out how to engage students in meaningful content in this environment, we have never done this before. Knowing that teachers learn best from each other and in teams, this element is more important than ever before.

We know that the most psychologically safe number of people in a group is two, though slightly larger can also work. As noted earlier, groups of six or more start to diminish in their effectiveness. In a virtual environment, this does not change. How can you have small teams of people working together in meaningful ways? How can you leverage technology for this practice?

As of this writing, Zoom and Microsoft Teams have a breakout feature that you can enable to be able to have staff move into small groups to dig into a given topic or project. My understanding is that GoogleMeet will have something similar in the near future.

The best resource I have seen to help facilitate learning in a virtual learning environment was created by the Washington State ASCD affiliate. The resource provides a description of tools and strategies, together with ideas for how to use the tool or strategy in a virtual environment. These tools work for both adult and student learning. You can find it here: http://wsascd.org/wp-content/uploads/Article_Virtual-Engagement-Strategies.pdf

---

Teacher Teams in Practice

Trang is in her second year as the principal of a middle school, grades six to eight, with roughly a thousand students. The school works hard to maintain a middle-level philosophy with students being on one team throughout the year. This means that a group of students has the same English, Math, Science, and Social Studies teachers for the whole year.

As part of the philosophy, teachers have two plan periods per day. One is a personal plan, and the other is a team plan. During her first year on the job, Trang noticed that the team plan time largely revolved around student problems. There was very little energy focused on improving professional practice, and meetings tended to devolve into sessions bemoaning student apathy, lack of parental involvement, and administrative micro-management.

During the fall of her first year, Trang simply observed the dynamics of teams. In the spring semester, though, she started building shared knowledge about effective teams. This included having teachers read articles on effective teaming and discussing the implications for their work. Additionally, she contacted nearby schools where she knew there were effective teams and sent representative staff members to observe their teams in action.

By April, Trang was ready to provide sample templates and timelines for the next school year for feedback from teams. The timeline included an expectation that one team plan day per week would focus on logistics of upcoming field trips, special events, and other managerial-type activities. One team plan day per week could be reserved for a focus on students—dealing with specific social, emotional, behavioral, or other issues to ensure the success of individual students with unique difficulties. The other three team plan days per week would be focused on professional learning that improved student learning.

Trang asked for all notes from team meetings to be submitted electronically to her. Additionally, specific work-products were expected from teams—such as common assessments, charts of data from those common assessments that included an emphasis on closing gaps, jointly developed lesson plans, examples of student work measured against common rubrics, etc. The proposed timeline laid these expectations out by date for the entire next year.

Fortunately, most staff were ready for the greater structure Trang was proposing for the meetings. However, there were a few staff members who lamented the additional proposed paperwork and requirements. Trang made sure to have these conversations in small group settings—with the teams—and not in entire staff meetings where a vocal minority could easily dominate and derail momentum toward greater effectiveness. She encouraged revisions to her proposed templates and timeline from staff.

At the beginning of the year, Trang brought back the revised templates and timelines from April. To assist with the organization of tasks, Trang provided all staff with a three-ring notebook with section dividers to hold materials for the year. Included in this binder were forms for feedback to the principal after each team meeting, protocols to assist with the work, examples of common assessments that prior-year teachers had used, and other materials necessary for the creation of a collaborative workplace environment for the teachers. Some tabs in the binder were pre-labeled (Norms, Feedback Forms, Assessments,

Data, Protocols), and others were left blank for teachers to use as they needed.

Finally, once per month, at the building staff meetings, Trang and the School Improvement Team provided just-in-time professional learning for the staff. Early on, they noticed a lack of authentic assessments being used to assess student learning. So in the September staff meeting, the School Improvement Team spent time on assisting staff with analyzing their student learning outcomes by "KRiSPing" them—an acronym for identifying if the outcome is Knowledge, Reasoning, Skill, or Product—for the kind of target (see Chapter Nine for a detailed discussion of KRiSP).

Staff then matched the type of evidence they would use (Selected Response, Extended Written Response, Teacher Observation, or Performance Task) to the kind of target. Finally, they developed common tools for assessing their outcomes. The KRiSPing and matching type of evidence were completed in the staff meeting, and the development of the assessment tool was started. Trang set the expectation for staff that one of their next team meetings should be focused upon the completion of that tool.

The teaching staff appreciated the focus of Trang in improving student learning—and the ability of their teams to focus on interdisciplinary skills. One of their complaints during the prior year was how IDUs—or Inter-Disciplinary Units—had gone away in the era of standardized testing. So the renewed focus on interdisciplinary outcomes energized new and veteran teachers, alike.

Staff also appreciated the organizational structure of a notebook to keep all of their materials in one place. While so much of our work is done digitally, having a physical and tangible notebook to refer to, take to meetings, and store everything in one place was particularly helpful. Of course, there was still grumbling from a minority of staff—and she dealt with it individually either directly or indirectly—depending on its impact on the process. In general, staff felt heard and supported because of the just-in-time learning at staff meetings. They understood how the work of school improvement was aligned with their practices, and how their practices were supporting school improvement. They felt valued, respected, and treated as professionals.

Finally, Trang made sure to attend at least one of the weekly collaborative planning time meetings per week—at least for a portion of the meeting. Her weekly update to staff highlighted specific teams' accomplishments, and she wrote handwritten notes to specific teams and teachers emphasizing excellence.

WANTING MORE?

Easton, L. B. (Ed.). (2015). *Powerful Designs for Professional Learning (3rd ed.).* Oxford, OH: Learning Forward.

Complete with a plethora of online tools, this resource is a must-have in developing effective teams. You'll find step-by-step processes, as well as a background of the research and theory for each of the 24 designs of professional learning. Further, you'll find a collection of websites and other resources to assist you with organizing effective teams.

Self-Assess and Apply Your Knowledge

Use the following table to self-assess your knowledge on each of the statements. Note how you go about bridging any knowing-doing gap in order to make each one a reality.

	I need to learn more	I know this	I can teach others	What I DO to make this happen
Use specific grouping strategies for teachers				
Teams of three to five				
Focus teams on improving instruction				
Have teachers **work** together				
Have teachers **plan** together				
Have teachers **think** together				
Have teachers **talk about professional issues** together				
Have teachers observe and respond to **teaching**				
Have teachers observe and respond to **curriculum**				
Have teachers observe and respond to **assessment**				
Have teachers develop **joint lesson plans**				
Have teachers develop **curriculum**				
Have teachers use protocols (step-by-step procedures for teams)				
Train teachers in the skills and knowledge of collaboration				
Use an incentive system for high teacher performance				
Eliminate the isolation of individual classrooms				
Network with teachers in other buildings and systems				

CHAPTER THREE

Staff Meetings

Elements of Principal Knowledge in Creating a Collaborative Workplace Environment for Teachers

To build a collaborative culture of professional learning, principals know and understand that:

3. Staff meetings should focus on learning and improvement
    A. Reduce or remove "adminis-trivia" from staff meetings
    B. Lambert's Tenets of Leadership

Focus on Learning

Designated leadership must focus on learning. This includes not only learning for students, but the learning of staff. As such, a prime time for engaging staff in their own professional learning is during staff meetings, which must shift from management and "adminis-trivia" to professional learning and improvement.

But let me be clear: management issues are fundamentally important to the effective functioning of a school. Building principals cannot ignore the pressing demands of staff leaves, transportation coordination, and the like. One of the quickest ways to being discredited is to ignore these issues, which can ultimately lead to logistical disasters. Rather, principals must use other means—besides staff meetings, to the greatest extent possible—to deal with these. This memo is an example of one such effort by an elementary principal.

Sample Memo to Staff
Courtesy of Lawrence Tunks, former principal at Alcott Elementary

SUBSTITUTE CALLING SYSTEM
In your mailbox, you will have a cheat sheet that you should take home. On it, it has directions on how to use it and it also has the phone number.

COMPENSATION TO COVER ANOTHER TEACHER'S CLASS
If you are covering another teacher's class and miss a plan period, you need to let an administrator know so you can be reimbursed.
If I tell you that you HAVE to do it, you will be reimbursed.
You can NOT get paid if you are covering someone's class if the other teacher does NOT fill out a leave.

PROFESSIONAL GROWTH FORMS
Must be submitted to me on March 1.
I believe these forms were handed out at the beginning of the year. If you do not have one, please let me know.

PLCS
If you miss a PLC for any reason, you must submit a leave form.

STATE TEST ACCOMMODATIONS
Third to fifth grade, SPED, and EL new accommodations are out. There have been some small changes. We need to meet sometime in the near future to discuss these accommodations, how to put them on IEPs, etc…

VIDEOS
If you are watching videos, they need to align with the curriculum that is being taught. Videos that are being watched must be critical to educational materials.
If you are watching a video as a reward for something that students accomplished, administrators must be notified.

So why is it important to focus staff meetings on staff learning? The ultimate goal is to create a collaborative workplace environment for teachers.

In a certain sense, collaboration can almost be seen as a "silver bullet" for improvement. As noted earlier, Lieberman and McLaughlin (1995, p. 66) highlighted the absolutely essential nature of collaboration in improving student learning by noting that involvement in collaborative activities "encourages exchange among the members [and] assures teachers that their knowledge of their students and of schooling is respected. Once they know this, they become committed to change, willing to take risks, and dedicated to self-improvement."

> **If effectiveness is what we want,
> then collaboration is what we need.**

To put it another way, if effectiveness is what we want, then collaboration is what we need. And creating a collaborative environment is enhanced by focusing staff meetings on staff learning.

In thinking about staff learning, let's visit Lambert's tenets of leadership for a bit, a subject that will be explored in more depth and with a slightly different twist in Chapter Eight. As part of this, think about how the implications of these tenets interact with the need to make staff meetings turn into learning meetings for staff.

This chapter is short because the knowledge for this element is relatively simple: turn your staff meetings into learning meetings for staff. So instead of spending your time reading a longer chapter on this topic, spend some time reflecting on Chart One. Use these questions to guide your reflection:

1) Which of these tenets am I most skillful in implementing?
2) Which of these tenets do I need to develop?
3) How might I go about developing this Knowledge/Skill?
4) How will I know that I've been successful in developing this Knowledge/Skill?

CHART 1

Lambert's Tenets of Leadership with key Knowledge, Skills, and Dispositions

	Knowledge	Skills	Dispositions
Tenet 1: Leadership does NOT equal leader	Leadership distribution Structures, systems, and processes	Leadership distribution Structures, systems, and processes	Belief in capacity of staff
Tenet 2: Leadership equals learning	Adult learning Student learning Adaptive vs. technical problems	Inventiveness Focus on continuous improvement of the system Dealing with adaptive and technical problems	Humility Learning High expectations Persistence
Tenet 3: All have the potential and right to work as leader	Effective grouping of staff Protocols	Implementation of team decisions Specific protocol use based on situation Providing time, encouraging, and expecting collaboration Facilitation of conversations	Trust of teachers Belief in power of collaboration Belief in decisions by teams
Tenet 4: Leading is a shared endeavor	Effective grouping of staff Protocols	Implementation of team decisions Specific protocol use based on situation Providing time, encouraging, and expecting collaboration Facilitation of conversations	Trust of teachers Belief in power of collaboration Belief and trust in decisions by teams
Tenet 5: Upside-down triangle of power	Where to involve staff in developing school policies and in providing input to important decisions	Facilitation of involvement and input	Belief in redistribution of power and authority Belief in teacher as instructional leader

Source: Dumas, 2010

Remote Learning Applications

Unsurprisingly, the element of staff meetings as learning meetings still applies in a remote learning environment. In many ways it becomes even more important to ensure that we're using this time well to maximize learning for students. Chapter One shared the importance of building relationships in this virtual environment, and Chapter Two mentioned some tools that can be helpful in creating such a safe environment for teachers to learn from and with each other. This chapter is really about making sure that you understand this principle, and then doing it. Imagine the following scenario, but in a remote learning environment—you'll find that it isn't that difficult to do.

Staff Meetings in Practice

Lenny is the principal of a three-section elementary school. Like many schools, there is a staff meeting once per month after school. These are typically one hour to one and a half hours long.

Staff fully understand that these meetings are not administrative in nature—some staff even refer to the meetings as "staff development meetings." They know that the focus will be on learning for the adults in the building to improve their practice so that student learning improves.

Lenny engages his School Improvement (SI) Team to plan all of the staff meetings so that he is not the sole leader in staff learning. Instead, the School Improvement Team plans the learning of staff in detail, and then facilitates the actual learning during the staff meeting. Sometimes the full team leads the staff in learning; other times they rotate responsibility for facilitating specific learning activities for the staff. Throughout all of the learning, though, it is clear that the SI Team members (including the principal) are co-learners with the staff. In this regard, they also call on members of the staff to facilitate some learning for the entire staff—ensuring that leadership capacity is built among all members of the staff.

Lenny's School Improvement Team is keenly aware of instructional best practice. They don't do worksheets with staff—just as they expect that staff minimize worksheets with students. Instead, they use strategies like modeling, guided practice, and independent practice. They use graphic organizers and note-taking techniques. They expect implementation of the learning at staff meetings, and have staff bring evidence of implementation to the next meeting, including evidence to show how the work is closing gaps for students. They create a culture of mutual accountability to each other, as opposed to up the chain of command to the building principal.

Staff meetings at Lenny's school are true learning meetings. They are a model for how classrooms should be run. Everyone knows this, and staff work to emulate this atmosphere in their classroom.

Self-Assess and Apply Your Knowledge

Use the following table to self-assess your knowledge on each of the statements. Note how you go about bridging any knowing-doing gap in order to make each one a reality.

	I need to learn more	I **know** **this**	I can teach others	What I DO to make this happen
Focus staff meetings on student learning				

CHAPTER FOUR

Principles of Adult Learning

Elements of Principal Knowledge in Creating a Collaborative Workplace Environment for Teachers

To build a collaborative culture of professional learning, principals know and understand:

4. **Principles of adult learning**
    A. External trainings are of limited usefulness because the challenge is to implement what is already known
    B. Characteristics of a Knowledge Worker
        1. Autonomy, complexity, and a connection between effort and reward
    C. Professional learning designs
        1. Assessment as professional learning
        2. Curriculum as professional learning
        3. Data analysis
        4. Lesson study
        5. Instructional coaching
        6. Professional learning communities
        7. Visual dialogue
    D. Job-embedded professional learning

Teachers Teaching Teachers

"One of the most frequently mentioned resources important to the effective functioning of a school is the professional development opportunities for teachers" (Marzano et al., 2005, p. 59). So professional development opportunities are an important resource—but not just any old professional development. We must hone in on *effective* practices of professional learning.

In this regard, and I cannot emphasize this enough, external trainings are of limited usefulness. Otherwise known as workshops or trainings, "old school" professional development will not improve student learning by itself. This is because the challenge of school improvement is largely to implement what is already known—not to create more knowledge. The challenge of school improvement is that of closing the knowing-doing gap.

> "Teachers do not learn best from outside experts or by attending conferences or implementing 'programs' installed by outsiders. Teachers learn best from other teachers, in settings where they literally teach each other the art of teaching."
> Schmoker, 2005, p. 141

Note that Schmoker (2005, p. 141) emphasizes that "teachers do not learn *best*" (emphasis added) in traditional forms of professional development. This does not mean that learning does not happen in traditional professional development. Many ideas and activities are learned and implemented at some level as a result of workshops, conferences, in-services, and trainings (a.k.a. traditional professional development). However, in comparison to traditional professional development, teachers learn *best* in job-embedded environments. The process of teachers teaching each other, supplemented by occasional external and traditional forms of professional development, has the greatest potential impact for creating a collaborative environment.

Schmoker (2005) speaks to the power of a new paradigm of professional development by emphasizing, quite emphatically, that the old system is outdated. "Another discovery that points to the timeliness and power of Professional Learning Communities is the emergent realization that training, though useful, is overrated and, in some cases, even unnecessary" (p. 147). Money, time, and energy are, in some cases, unnecessary, and can be saved and diverted toward actual improvement of student learning.

Think of how expensive it is to bring an "expert" into a district. A decent speaker can cost anywhere from $3,000 per day (plus expenses) to upwards of $10,000 per day (plus expenses). This is *per day*. Or consider how much it costs to send staff to a conference. Most conferences are around $800 for registration alone—then there's the cost of transportation, food, lodging, and more. In total sending one person to a conference is typically around $2,000 or more.

Schmoker says that these expenses are overrated, at best, and possibly even unnecessary. These dollars can be re-allocated to improve instruction. They can be re-directed toward high-quality professional learning—job-embedded professional learning—that will actually impact professional practice that will improve student learning. The resources can be directed toward putting the "C" into PLC: when you build a collaborative community, teachers will learn from each other.

Though the research is clear on this point—we have half a century of evidence leading to this conclusion—it doesn't mean that you can easily transition to truly powerful professional learning where teachers are teaching each other. The easy way is to go to a speaker and laugh for a few hours. This is much easier than getting together with colleagues and planning curriculum, instruction, and assessment. It is easier to listen to best-practice or research than to change one's own practice. The easy way is to listen to an inspirational speaker tell how much of an impact you are having on the lives of students—much easier than making deep changes to one's practice so that an even more meaningful impact can be had on students' lives.

Most professionals love going to conferences. I, personally, love going to conferences. It's a really important part of my own professional life—so much so that I have personally paid to attend the Learning Forward Annual Conference. It's fulfilling to me, personally and professionally, and it's the one and only conference that I prioritize going to each year.

At conferences, I get to go to workshops. I get to network. I get free stuff from vendors. I feel really good and energized about my work. I'm downright excited each time I come home from a conference.

But it takes a great deal of self-discipline to come home and actually look at my notes and review my learning periodically after the conference. It takes a great deal of energy not to fall into the same old day-to-day practices. The actual work of improving my practice to improve student learning will not happen in those workshops or trainings.

The work of improving my practice typically comes by way of me teaching others. So it is with teachers: the work of improving their practice comes by way of teachers teaching teachers. This is about walking a path of learning together. It doesn't imply expert or novice; all can teach and all can learn. This is the hard way. But it's also the way that will actually help kids improve their lives.

Job-embedded Professional Learning

There is almost unparalleled consensus in the education world about the necessity for job-embedded professional learning. The message is clear: designated leadership is a vital necessity for changing the culture of a school from isolated, independent contractors to a unified system of colleagues working systematically for the improvement of student learning. Be that leader.

A system of colleagues working together does not mean that all teachers are robotic and doing the exact same thing. Teaching to standards does not mean standardization. What it means is that staff are working together, integrating techniques and ideas from their own and different content areas. It might mean co-teaching. Or it might mean collaborating about the same fiction from reading integrated with social studies and English. And it includes co-laboring with art, music, and PE—as these can be very powerful supporters in improving student learning. A system means that staff are coordinating their instruction, not doing the same thing.

As a couple of examples, I've seen powerful ways in which PE teachers coordinate their instruction with reading. On the gymnasium wall are sight words or spelling words to which students run as part of warm-ups. Or music teachers who work with upper elementary teachers to coordinate songs and instruments with the literature being studied—like "Follow the Drinkin' Gourd" when studying the Underground Railroad.

Examples like these can be indicators of a coordinated system working to improve student learning.

Returning to job-embedded professional learning and juxtaposing the limited usefulness of external trainings with the notion that teachers learn best from each other, this creates a solid foundation for the importance of job-embedded professional learning. So what is job-embedded professional learning? Mullen & Hutinger (2008) define it as "learning activities that occur during work hours and that support instructional needs."

Pfeffer and Sutton, business gurus focused on the knowing-doing gap, take this concept one step further. They state that success "depends largely on *implementing what is already known* rather than from adopting new or previously unknown ways of doing things" (emphasis added, Pfeffer & Sutton, 1999, p. 88).

So it is not that the old paradigm of professional development simply compacts itself into mini-trainings, workshops, or conferences, per se. Rather, the job-embedded paradigm focuses primarily on "implementing what is already known," and the best way to implement what is already known is by creating a collaborative culture of professional learning. Be the designated leader who helps teachers implement what they already know.

Educators: The Ultimate Knowledge Worker

Educators are the ultimate knowledge worker. Not only must we be in command of our content, instructional practices, assessment practices, classroom management techniques—the list goes on—but we are ultimately in charge of passing on knowledge to the next generation. If our work is not that of a knowledge worker, then I don't know what is.

The term *knowledge worker* was coined by Peter Drucker, one of the leading experts on management. According to Drucker (1999, p. 135), "The most important, and indeed the truly unique, contribution of management in the 20th Century was the fifty-fold increase in the productivity of the MANUAL WORKER in manufacturing. The most important contribution management needs to make in the 21st Century is similarly to increase the productivity of KNOWLEDGE WORK and the KNOWLEDGE WORKER."

> "Knowledge workers...don't like to be told what to do. Thinking for a living engenders thinking for oneself. Knowledge workers are paid for their education, experience, and expertise, so it is not surprising that they take offense when someone else rides roughshod over their intellectual territory."
> Thomas Davenport, *Thinking for a Living*, 2005, p. 15

In order to be successful, a knowledge worker must have several conditions: autonomy, complexity, and a connection between effort and reward.

Regarding autonomy, this does not mean that educators must be allowed to do whatever they want, whenever they want. We are not a collection of private contractors within the buildings that we serve. We are interconnected, and the entire purpose of this book is to spell out the knowledge that a principal must possess in order to create such interdependence in their building.

Rather, autonomy to a knowledge worker means that the responsibility for productivity is on the individual. In the case of education, that productivity manifests itself in student learning. So responsibility for this student learning is not with parents, the community, blamed on demographics or any other factor. Responsibility for student learning is on us—and we must manage ourselves to improve that student learning.

A second aspect of a knowledge worker is the importance of complexity in their work. The job cannot be menial, by rote, or doing the same thing from day to day. A culture of innovation (or innovativeness) has to be present in order for the knowledge worker to feel successful. Chapter Five will discuss this topic.

Finally, and related to the idea of complexity, is that the efforts of a knowledge worker must involve continuous learning—coupled with a connection between effort and reward. We are not satisfied with doing the same thing over and over again—but instead need to be involved in continuous learning so that we can innovate. And in order to continuously improve, we need to be able to see that our efforts are paying off—not in terms of financial gain, as important as this might be, but in terms of improved productivity. The real motivator is student success, results in the classroom, students who can continue on their path of learning because of what happened in the classroom. The ultimate productivity in our field is improved student learning.

The days of teachers recycling the same unchanged lesson plans year after year are over. Lessons must be changed, tweaked, and maybe even thrown out if they don't fit what the team has decided is essential for student learning. For some, this may be really hard. For others, refreshing. For some tips on facilitating change and sustaining that change, please see Chapter 10.

Not only are these principles of success important for educators, but they are a foundational principle in the most unlikely of places: the assembly line. A few years ago, I was touring an assembly line factory that makes air conditioners for large vehicles. As part of the tour, the management was explaining their practices of improvement—basically PDSA (Plan, Do, Study, Act) from Deming (1986).

During the tour, we were encouraged to ask questions—like how they go about improvement, how they measure improvement, and how they engage the workers in improvement. Finally, at one point, the manager turned to us and said, "Don't tell them, but they really don't need us in order for them to do their job. Our job, as managers, is to build their capacity to make the improvements on their own."

I was dumbfounded. "Our job is to build their capacity to make improvements." This was on a factory floor. The workers were high school educated. And their job was to put screws in holes and tighten them—all day long. And the job of management is to build capacity.

How much more, then, is our job as leaders in the education field to build the capacity of teachers: the greatest Knowledge Workers on the planet?!

Professional Learning Designs

The principal must be knowledgeable about learning—for both adults and students—and must possess the skills necessary to create an atmosphere of learning. Fortunately, Easton (2015) identified two dozen designs for powerful professional learning. Please see Chapter Two for a deeper exploration of seven of these designs—those most critical for putting the "C" in PLC.

The use of these designs of professional learning will greatly assist in creating collaborative learning communities and promoting shared leadership. Their use facilitates data collection and analysis, including the use of multiple sources of information to guide and show improvement. Further, they facilitate research-based decision-making and help to access what we know about how students learn. Finally, they provide us with the skills and knowledge to collaborate effectively.

Teachers yearn for opportunities to collaborate—where the focus is on doing, not just knowing. But, like all of us, they need more than simple encouragement—they need structures and expectations to facilitate this collaboration, designs like those mentioned by Easton and enumerated in Chapter Two. The principal plays the primary role in facilitating an environment for this job-embedded professional learning.

Remote Learning Applications

During COVID-19, with travel severely limited, the application of this principle has been (and I suspect will continue to be) fairly straightforward. With face-to-face conferences and trainings being canceled, it appears that our profession is gaining a better understanding that teachers learn best in teams, that learning designs are necessary, and that we have a plethora of resources outside of our previously limited thinking around professional development.

While many conferences have simply gone online, we have realized the power of learning from each other through social media and other platforms. Within a very short period of time of school building closures, the notion that we are living in an information age became glaringly obvious. A few resources that may be helpful:

- https://sites.google.com/esc16.net/distance-learning-playbook/home

- https://partnership4success.org/equity
- https://createforeducation.org/sel-consulting/rebuilding-community/
- https://teachfromhome.google/intl/en/

> ### Principles of Adult Learning in Practice
>
> Keisha is the principal of a three-section elementary school. Understanding the needs of adult learners, Keisha structures staff meetings, collaborative team meetings, and professional development days around the learning needs of staff. She emphasizes the implementation of research-based and best practices.
>
> Keisha works with the District Office to ensure that any speakers brought into the District for professional development align with the initiatives in the District, and that these speakers are only once per year unless part of a sustained process of ongoing coaching and follow-up. She knows that staff must have time to plan for the implementation of their learning from District-initiated speakers, and having more than one external expert per year would generally not meet that criteria. She regularly discusses the knowing-doing gap in friendly terms, and reminds colleagues that their emphasis is always on implementing what they already know.
>
> In her interactions with staff, she highlights the professional autonomy of teachers to make appropriate decisions to improve student learning. She occasionally prods their work by providing targeted articles, chapters from books, or video clips that will enhance the innovation of her staff—and/or ensure that they remain focused on implementing research-based or best practice.
>
> To meet the need of a knowledge worker to see the results of their efforts, Keisha prominently displays data throughout the building. For example, data from walkthroughs with percent of students on-task, or objectives posted, or student-friendly data displayed in classrooms—all of this evidence is tracked, posted in the office/teacher workroom, disaggregated by subgroups to

ensure inequities are being identified, and celebrated at staff meetings or other opportunities.

In her work with the School Improvement Leadership Team, Keisha provides examples of the professional designs discussed in Chapter Two (Curriculum as professional learning, Assessment as professional learning, Data analysis, Lesson study, Instructional coaching, Professional learning communities, and Visual dialogue). The Leadership Team then makes intentional decisions about which designs they use to assist staff with implementing their Action Plan. For example, as they begin the year, they want staff to think critically about how they assess student learning. So they focus on quality assessment practices using backwards design—identifying the target and designating it as Knowledge, Reasoning, Skill, or Product, then selecting or developing the appropriate assessment tool based on the target—Selected Response, Extended Written Response, Performance Task, or Teacher Observation. Later on, after pre-assessment results roll in, the Leadership Team focuses staff learning on Data Analysis protocols to assist with the Lesson Design.

Throughout the year, Keisha reminds her staff of the importance of job-embedded professional learning. She also ensures that all staff meetings, staff development days, and collaborative team meetings are focused on professional learning. Her focus is on implementation—making sure that staff are actually doing what they are learning. And she provides regular evidence to staff of the impact on student learning that they are having with closing the knowing-doing gap.

In all of this work, staff are learning. They are grappling with protocols, wrapping their heads around Lesson Design, examining data, and more. This is how learning works, and it's okay. Try something, learn how it works, then do it better next time. And then better the next time. And then better the next time.

In the beginning, everyone only has a basic idea of what to do. Keisha assures staff that the greatest mistake is to do nothing. Do something. Try. Do the best right now and then your best will get better next time.

And so it goes for you, too. As you learn about these principles, put them into practice. Learn by doing. As you do, you will become clearer and more refined in your thinking. And the cycle will continue.

WANTING MORE?

Learning Forward. (2011). *Standards for Professional Learning.* Oxford, OH: Learning Forward.

The most recent in a series of revisions of Standards for Staff Development over the past several decades. Learning Forward puts forth seven standards for professional learning—the name of the standards, itself, denotes a shift in thinking about professional learning from one-day wonders to a continuous process.

Learning Forward. (2012). *Standards into Practice: School-based Roles. Innovation Configuration Maps for Standards for Professional Learning.* Oxford, OH: Learning Forward.

The seven standards of professional learning are brought to life by Innovation Configuration (IC) Maps. An IC map is, in a nutshell, a fancy term for a rubric—the main differences being that an IC Map does not designate levels of performance that are equidistant, nor are there artificial distinctions placed between levels of performance.

The important point of IC Maps is that they designate very specific actions that one must take to get to higher and higher levels of performance. These IC Maps clarify what a principal must know/do, school leadership teams must know/do, coaches must know/do, and what individual teachers must know/do in order to adhere to these standards. The IC Maps are helpful in identifying current practice and then planning for higher levels of implementation.

Easton, L. B. (Ed.). (2015). *Powerful Designs for Professional Learning (3rd ed.).* Oxford, OH: Learning Forward.

Complete with a set of tools, this resource is a must-have in developing effective teams. You'll find step-by-step processes, as well as a background of the research and theory for each of the 24 designs of professional learning. You'll also find a collection of websites and other resources to assist you with organizing effective teams.

Self-Assess and Apply Your Knowledge

Use the following table to self-assess your knowledge on each of the statements. Note how you go about bridging any knowing-doing gap in order to make each one a reality.

Adult Learning Principles	I need to learn more	I know this	I can teach others	What I DO to make this happen
Principals must have teachers work together in teams as the best way to improve student learning				
Principals must engage teachers in daily professional learning as the best way to improve student learning				

Designs of Professional Learning	I need to learn more	I know this	I can teach others	What I DO to make this happen
Developing, scoring, interpreting, and acting on **assessments** as professional learning				
Designing, implementing, reflecting on, and revising **curriculum** as professional learning				
Analyzing and acting on **data** as professional learning				
Engaging in lesson **study** as professional learning				
Engaging in faculty **Professional Learning Communities** as				

CHAPTER FIVE

Continuous Improvement and Innovation

Elements of Principal Knowledge in Creating a Collaborative Workplace Environment for Teachers

To build a collaborative culture of professional learning, principals know and understand that:

5. **Continuous improvement is necessary. Effective elements include:**
   A. Focusing resources on a small number of goals
   B. Data collection and analysis
   C. The use of multiple sources to guide and demonstrate improvement
   D. Research-based decision-making
   E. A simple focus on refining processes in small ways
   F. Clear, frequent talk about instruction
   G. Recognition and celebration for superior practices and results
   H. Inventiveness/innovativeness where risk-taking is encouraged
   I. High expectations for learning
   J. Using groups as the main units for improvement

Creating a collaborative workplace environment is not just a lofty ideal. It involves the application of the specific knowledge discussed throughout this book. It requires skillful school and district leaders, and it involves an understanding of continuous improvement and what it takes for innovativeness.

Continuous improvement and innovation are not about doing whatever you want, whenever you want to do it. There are specific processes and steps that are necessary for continuous improvement and innovation to be effective.

Leadership = Learning

Continuous improvement and innovation are fundamentally about learning. In order to improve and to innovate, we must be willing to learn. As the saying goes, if we always do what we've always done, then we'll always get what we've always gotten.

Deming delineates the key difference between leadership and management as being how the leader responds to needs. In order to be successful, leadership must focus on continuous improvement and innovation—as opposed to purely management. One implication of this work on the system, as a whole, is that the focus must be on the learning of individuals within the system.

Less Is More: A Few Goals Based on Data

Less is more. When we try to do too many things, we end up doing nothing. It is far better to have a small number of goals and to do them well than to have a bunch of goals and do a myriad of activities that may or may not improve student learning.

But don't confuse few with easy. Goals must be lofty, as high expectations for learning must be the norm. Lezotte's Correlates of Effective Schools states that high expectations for students are critical for improving student learning. Don't succumb to the pressure of setting *attainable* goals. Set stretch goals, possibly out of reach. If you set low goals, you will probably attain them. If you set high goals, you may not reach them—but you'll likely achieve higher and better results than if you set low goals. Just like with kids.

Goals must be based on data. The days of supposition, hunch feelings, and perception-based goals are over. The days of data-informed decision-making are here to stay.

Notice that I used the phrase "data-informed." You can also use the term "data-based." However, I never use the term "data-driven." This is because data should never *drive* our decisions—we, as professionals, should drive our decisions. We should use data to *inform* our professional judgment. Otherwise, we are mere robots who are mindlessly following calculations from data without sorting through it to come to professional judgments upon which decisions and actions are based.

There are a number of different types of data to inform decision-making. In its most simple form, there are four types: Student achievement, Demographic, Program, and Perception data. Using all four types of data in determining goal areas for the building will lead to goal(s) that are high-leverage; a goal based on all four of these types of data will positively impact student learning.

1. Achievement data tells us **how well students are doing** and includes **Norm-Referenced Tests, Criterion-Referenced Tests, IEP achievement data, report card grades, Advanced Placement, ACT and SAT scores, etc.**
2. Demographic data tells us **who the students are** and includes **gender, race, ethnicity, socio-economic status (SES), mobility, English Learners, suspension and expulsion rates, special education, etc.**
3. Program data tells us **who the teachers are and what the curriculum is** and includes **instructional program data, professional development data, school organization data, parental involvement data, staff data, etc.**
4. Perception data tells us **how people feel about the school** and includes **surveys, student and staff wellness and absenteeism info, discipline reports, parent/community volunteerism, etc.**

Good Goals vs. Bad Goals

As you go about setting your one to three goals that will last over the course of three to five years, how will you know what is a good goal and what is a bad goal? Is there such a thing as a good goal and a bad goal? And how do you tell the difference?

In its most simple form, a good goal is one that will get folks moving toward improving professional practice that improves student learning. A bad goal is one that sits on the shelf and does nothing to improve teacher practice, and, thus, student learning. Unfortunately, there are a lot of bad goals in schools…

So setting a goal, and the language of that goal, is not as important as *how* you get to that goal. How do you engage staff in conversations around data? How do you gain consensus toward the goal? How do you celebrate movement toward the attainment of that goal? Other chapters of this book deal with these questions specifically—what you must know is that the goal, by itself, is not necessarily good or bad. It's how the goal moves the school toward improving student learning that matters.

For example, improving reading in all curricular areas is a pretty important goal in schools across the country these days. Reading is a high-leverage goal—it impacts all learning. It's also enduring—students will need to read throughout their life. Finally, it's cross-curricular—students need to read in a variety of settings in order to be successful.

So improving reading could be a pretty good goal. But there are many schools that are beyond simply improving reading. Their data shows high performance in this area—so they may be focused on 21st Century Skills (https://www.battelleforkids.org/networks/p21): Collaboration, Communication, Creativity, and Critical Thinking. For a school focused on any of these four Cs, a goal in reading would be a bad goal. Their data does not support it, staff would likely not be able to come to consensus on it, and it definitely would not improve the practice of teachers to improve student learning. In this case, reading is a bad goal.

What about behavioral goals? For example, stopping bullying or decreasing classroom interruptions. We all know that learning does not occur unless classrooms are orderly environments. However, focusing solely on student behavior will not improve teacher practice that improves student learning. While a behavior goal may be a necessary antecedent in your school, it cannot replace academic learning goals. The academic learning goals are where you'll see true changes in teacher practice and improvement in student learning. I've seen it happen in more than one place where teachers will have their students so focused on learning that kids won't have time or gumption to mess around!

A Few Goals: Now What?

Once you have a small number of goals—one to three—it is important to then focus resources on them. Just because you have a few goals doesn't mean that you'll be effective. Those goals must be supported by resources.

The most common form of allocating resources toward goals is the use of an Action Plan. There are many types of action plans that can be used—the important point is to *use* one. Whatever the format, an action plan is not worth the paper it is written on unless it drives action. The action plan needs to be just that—a *plan* for driving action. It's not a pretty document, or one that sits on a shelf, or one that simply gets dates changed every year. Rather, it is a living and breathing document that directs all of your School Improvement work.

When the action plan is being developed, it is critical that the actions in the plan are research- or evidence-based. Don't waste your time on potentially useless actions. Instead, invest your energy on developing, and then doing, a plan that is based on what works. My experience is that this research and consensus-building typically takes many months to up to a year to do well.

The following chart provides some sample resources that you could reference as part of developing your action plan. These are all based on the idea that the primary intervention is that of building capacity of the individuals in the organization to improve student learning. This is not an exhaustive set, but rather a starting point for thinking about how to increase the capacity of you and your colleagues to improve student learning.

Here is a template for a typical Continuous Improvement Action Plan. A complete example is provided later in this chapter.

Sample School Action Plan
Sample School

Target Area for Improvement:

Improvement Goal:	Expectations for Student Learning:	Targeted Participants:
Intervention:		Evaluation:

Timeframe for Implementation:

Actions	Schedule	Responsibilities	Monitoring	Resources
Year 1:				
Year 2:				
Year 3:				

CHART 2
A Menu of Resources for Activities

Based on the Intervention:
Building the capacity of individuals in the organization to improve student learning

Instructional	Other Stakeholders
International Center for Leadership in Education *The ICLE has developed a wealth of tools around Rigor/Relevance/Relationships, Learning Criteria, and effective leadership.*	
Results, Results Now, and Focus *An outline of the essential elements of instruction that are necessary to radically improve student learning.*	**Building Engaged Schools** *Based on Gallup's Research on Hope, Wellbeing, and Engagement, Gordon identifies specific steps schools can take to increase the levels of engagement of students, teachers, and communities.*
Adaptive Schools *The goal of Adaptive Schools is to develop our collective identity and capacity as collaborators, inquirers, and leaders. The purpose is to support staff in developing and facilitating efficacious, thoughtful, collaborative groups.*	**The 7 Habits of Highly Effective People** and **The 8 Habits of Highly Effective Teens** *A synopsis of the knowledge, skills, and habits necessary to be effective and great.*
Visible Learning *Visible Learning means an enhanced role for teachers as they become evaluators of their own teaching. According to John Hattie, Visible Learning and Teaching occurs when teachers see learning through the eyes of students and help them become their own teachers.*	**The Leader in Me** *Based on Covey's 7 Habits, this process teaches leadership skills to children and staff by creating a common language and set of principles used by staff, students, and parents (Designed for Elementary).*
Quantum Learning *Based on brain research, a set of principles for lesson design and specific activities for engaging students in meaningful learning and life-skill activities.*	**Whale Done!** *The application of 1) Build Trust, 2) Accentuate the Positive, and 3) Redirect When Mistakes Occur to achieve greater productivity and results.*
Reading Next *A follow-up to ReadingFirst, the findings highlight 15 elements that are key to any effective literacy program for adolescent students (grades four to eight).*	**National PTO Organization** *www.ptotoday.com has a wealth of tools and resources for engaging students, parents, and community members in improving student learning.*
Silent Sustained Reading (SSR) *Marzano outlines the five steps necessary to create a wide reading and language experience at a school.*	
Classroom Instruction That Works *The authors examined decades of research findings to distill the results into nine categories of teaching strategies that have positive effects on student learning.*	
How People Learn *A "How To" guide from the National Research Council on necessary effective elements of instruction based on brain research.*	
High Schools That Work and **Making Middle Grades Work** *Provides a framework of Goals, Key Practices, and Key Conditions for accelerating learning and setting higher standards. It recommends research-based practices for schools to improve academic and career/technical instruction and student achievement.*	

ADDITIONAL RESOURCES FOR POTENTIAL INTERVENTIONS:
https://www.rand.org/pubs/tools/TL145.html
The Promising Practices Network (PPN) site highlights programs and practices that credible research indicates are effective in improving outcomes for children, youth, and families. The information offered is organized around three major areas: Proven and Promising Programs, Research in Brief, and Strengthening Service Delivery.

https://ies.ed.gov/ncee/wwc/
On an ongoing basis, the What Works Clearinghouse (WWC) collects, screens, and identifies studies of the effectiveness of educational interventions (programs, products, practices, and policies). They review the studies that have the strongest design, and report on the strengths and weaknesses of those studies against the WWC Evidence Standards so that you know what the best scientific evidence has to say.

http://www.colorado.edu/cspv/blueprints/index.html
Blueprints has identified 17 model programs that have proven efficacy, and 76 that show promise and deserve additional research.

https://campbellcollaboration.org/evidence-portals.html
The Campbell Collaboration consists of two unique systems: portals and databases. According to their site: "Evidence portals are websites which present research evidence in a form accessible to policy makers and practitioners. A good portal is easy to navigate, with clearly defined interventions, presenting the best available evidence on the most cost effective approaches to achieving the desired outcomes. The portal should provide links to the underlying research."

"An evidence database provides links to rigorous reviews and primary studies, often allowing searching by sector and country. In an evidence portal this evidence has been further translated by the portal manager to make it more accessible. Evidence portals are aimed at consumers of evidence. Evidence databases may be used by consumers, but are also useful for producers of evidence synthesis as part of their search."

http://www.evidencebasedprograms.org/
U.S. social programs are often implemented with little regard to rigorous evidence, costing billions of dollars yet failing to address critical needs of our society—in areas such as education, crime and substance-abuse policy, and poverty reduction. A key piece of the solution, they believe, is to provide policymakers and practitioners with clear, actionable information on what works, as demonstrated in scientifically valid studies, that can be used to improve life outcomes.

https://www.wilsonlanguage.com/wp-content/uploads/2015/04/buildingreadingproficiencysecondary.pdf
Building Reading Proficiency at the Secondary Level: A Guide to Resources from the Southwest Educational Development Library.

https://ctl.uoregon.edu/
The University of Oregon Center on Teaching and Learning has a plethora of research- and evidence-based resources and analyses to inform school improvement, program implementation, and curriculum planning.

Simple Improvement

In the business world, Collins (2001) refers to continuous improvement as having a simple focus on improving processes in small but innumerable and incremental ways. It is not about having grandiose plans, or complex strategies, or expensive consultants, or time-consuming trainings. It is improvement, plain and simple.

Though action plans are for improvement—these provide an overarching picture of where you're heading and a three- to five-year plan of what needs to be accomplished—the long and short of continuous improvement is in the details of little improvements. As the saying goes, "Rome was not built in a day." Neither are significant improvements in teaching and learning made overnight. Instead, you have to tweak and adjust and modify and revise—all the little things—to accomplish continuous improvement. And this means that you have to pay attention to how things are unfolding and progressing in your building.

As part of a simple focus on improving processes in innumerable and incremental ways, it's vital that the building leadership engages in clear, frequent talk about instruction with teachers. What are you seeing in classrooms? What are best practices that you should be seeing in classrooms? Maybe more fundamentally than these questions is, "Are you in classrooms?"

You cannot have clear and frequent discussions about instruction if you don't know what is happening in your building. As you become aware of specific instructional techniques that staff are using, talk about them. Discuss them. Use these discussions about instruction as the center of your conversations with staff.

As you are discussing instruction with staff, it will become easy to recognize and celebrate excellence. Celebrations establish our culture—what we value, honor, and commemorate. So celebrate quality instruction. Make it public so that staff, students, parents, and the community know what's happening with instruction. Make instruction the centerpiece of your school.

> Over my career I have had many opportunities to spend significant chunks of time in buildings with teachers and principals. One particular set of interactions was especially powerful as I was determined to spend just about every moment of my day in classrooms, hallways, and the cafeteria. Because I was in classrooms, even for brief moments of time, and because I was intentional about following up with teachers about specific students after behavioral issues, we were able to have significant conversations about teaching and learning.
>
> One interaction was particularly memorable. A student had had issues the previous afternoon, and I just went to the teacher, prior to school starting, and asked how the rest of the afternoon had gone with this student. The fact that it didn't go well wasn't the point of my interacting with her—it was an opportunity to talk about her instructional practices and how she was meeting

the needs of her students (including this one). What resulted was not only an opportunity for her to feel validated and honored as a professional (I deliberately used the 3 + 1 moves noted in Chapter One), but for us to spend about five minutes talking about her instructional moves, what had worked and what hadn't, and how she might adjust her practices to meet this student's needs. While the start of the conversation was about a student's behavior, the heart of the dialogue was about instruction—the centerpiece of our schools.

Innovativeness

Research-based decision-making is important for continuous improvement. And so is innovativeness. These two ideas might seem contradictory: research-based decision-making and innovativeness. Research-based decision-making implies that what you are doing is tried and true. It works. We know it works. On the other hand, innovativeness implies trying new things—innovating. It means that you don't really, for sure, know that what you're trying is going to work.

But both are necessary for continuous improvement. How can that be?

Notice the use of the term "innovativeness"—not innovation. Innovativeness is a process—it is action oriented in a systematic, continuous improvement process. It implies the creation of a *culture* of innovation and innovativeness (Fullan, 2020). It implies a climate where risk-taking is encouraged. Not only might that risk-taking be encouraged, but it is even expected.

Innovation, on the other hand, is typically a one-time event or product. Unfortunately, innovation can be a one-time event multiplied over and over and over again. This, as you can imagine, creates innovation fatigue—which leads to a lack of implementation and meaningful improvement. In other words, innovation, devoid of a culture of innovativeness where there is a process of continuous improvement—will fail to improve student learning.

So, yes, research-based decision-making *and* innovativeness are both important for improving student learning.

Sit 'n' Git vs. Git 'r' Done

One final point regarding continuous improvement: sit 'n' git, especially when the presenter simply comes in and is never seen again, won't work. I have heard some leaders say that when we bring everyone together to hear the same thing that we are all on the same page—but it doesn't work that way. Each of us hears the same words, but our interpretations of those same words are filtered by our unique knowledge and life experiences. Hence, just because everyone hears the same thing does not mean that they *understand* the same thing. And the theory of being on the same page as a result is inaccurate. Getting on the same page comes through doing similar work together as you and staff learn by doing.

As noted in Chapter Four, now is the time for small groups of staff to work on implementing the professional learning of your school, supplemented by external expertise (when appropriate) and with systematic follow-up for implementation and coaching. For a full discussion of teaming of teachers, refer to Chapter Two. For the sake of understanding continuous improvement, know that teams of teachers are where the improvement happens—not in full staff meetings.

Continuous Improvement and Innovation in Practice (including Remotely)

Juan is the principal of an elementary school with 700 students. As part of the District's improvement process, the school has focused its energy on improving literacy. The school, as a whole, came to this goal area as their focus after a number of faculty meetings and planning-period meetings led by School Improvement Team members. Staff decided that improving literacy was a much more high-leverage goal than simply improving reading. Literacy, they contended, was important in every content area, and could be a focus for every staff member in the building. So improving literacy was their one and only goal.

The School Improvement (SI) Team—consisting of a teacher from each grade level as well as support teachers—meets once per month after school for about an hour. The co-chairs of the SI Team and the building principal meet at least every other week for about an hour to prepare for the full team meetings. They want to make sure that every SI Team meeting is as productive as possible as they plan for monthly staff development (or professional development) meetings. (Juan does not refer to staff meetings as staff meetings—but as staff development meetings.)

The SI Team developed an action plan to guide their work during the next three years. Because it is a guide, it will likely change as they move through implementation. As such, you will notice that the first year is much more detailed than subsequent years.

The focus of staff learning is on Marzano's Instructional Framework: *The Art and Science of Teaching* (2007). This is a multi-year focus where each year identifies a specific aspect of this research-based instructional framework. Groups of teachers—each grade-level team—focus on improving their instruction through the implementation of the instructional framework. An instructional coach helps with gathering data as well as assisting teachers with implementation of their learning. Data for implementation is collected on an ongoing basis by the building principal, and student learning improvements are monitored throughout the school year.

82   LET'S PUT THE C IN PLC

Here is an example of an action plan that was promised earlier. By the end of this plan, this particular school was recognized as a national model for improving student performance. It was and is a high-poverty, high-diversity school, and, thanks to the work of this principal and staff, is also a high-performing school.

CHART 3
Revised based on the work of Montessa Muñoz, former principal at Lincoln Elementary

Lincoln School Action Plan
Sample Public Schools

Target Area for Improvement: Reading Kindergarten: (Phonemic Awareness, Phonological Awareness, Word Analysis); First: (Phonological Awareness, Phonics); Second: (Word Analysis)

Improvement Goal: Long-term: 90% of K-2 students will be at benchmark according to DIBELS Next composite score by May of Year 3. Short-term: 70% of K-2 students will be at benchmark according to DIBELS Next composite scores by May of Year 1.	Expectations for Student Learning: Students will be able to read fluently from various texts.	Targeted Participants: All K-2 students

Intervention: Curriculum: Identify opportunities and strategies in Treasures and Working With Words (WWW) to reinforce the development of reading strategies and concepts taught during whole group reading. Assessment: Align opportunities and strategies found in Treasures and Working With Words to skills tested using DIBELS Next. Convene staff development to train faculty on assessing students on DIBELS. Incorporate staff developments to train faculty on what DIBELS benchmarks are and how to utilize that data to drive instructional strategies. Instruction: Implement Marzano's *The Art and Science of Teaching* (2007).

Evaluation: DIBELS Next assessment three times a year. Rigby K-2

Timeframe for Implementation: 1-4 years

Actions	Schedule	Responsibilities	Monitoring	Resources
Year 1:				
Train and implement the communication of learning goals, track student progress, and celebrate success (Ch. 1).	August, Year 1	Principal overview 1 week before school starts; train staff and meet with grade levels 1xmo. Teachers will work on answering What will I do to establish and communicate learning goals, track student progress, and celebrate success? (PLC: Q1,2) Instructional Facilitator will aid teachers in reflecting and implementing new practices.	Principal will assess new learning through walkthroughs using Marzano's Observational Protocol. Walkthrough data monitored monthly. Track class progress 3xyr. Teacher-created scales, and class tracking graphs.	*The Art and Science of Teaching*. Weekly/bi-weekly grade level meetings. Examples of scales and tracking sheets.
Helping students effectively interact with new knowledge (Ch. 2).	August, Year 1	Principal overview 1 week before school starts; train staff and meet with grade levels 1xmo. Teachers will work on answering What will I do to help my student interact with new knowledge? (PLC: Q1) Instructional Facilitator will aid teachers in reflecting and implementing new practices.	Principal will assess new learning through walkthroughs using Marzano's Observational Protocol. Walkthrough data monitored monthly Track class progress 3xyr.	*The Art and Science of Teaching*. Weekly/bi-weekly grade level meetings.

Actions	Schedule	Responsibilities	Monitoring	Resources
Engaging students (Ch. 5).	August, Year 1	Principal overview 1 week before school starts; train staff and meet with grade levels 1xmo. Teachers will work on answering What will I do to engage new students? (PLC: Q1). Instructional Facilitator will aid teachers in reflecting on and implementing new practices.	Principal will assess new learning through walkthroughs using Marzano's Observational Protocol. Walkthrough data monitored monthly. Track class progress 3xyr.	*The Art and Science of Teaching.* Weekly/bi-weekly grade level meetings.
Identify and align how phonics/ phonological awareness are taught across grades K-2 (concepts, strategies, resources by grade level).	Sept to May, Year 1	Instructional Facilitator will observe WWW lessons. Instructional Facilitator will work with SI team and grade-level teams to ensure alignment of concepts, strategies, and resources.	Alignment spreadsheet	Alignment spreadsheet, time during SI meetings, WWW scope and sequence.
Identify what assessment data will be shared, how often, and by whom with grade-level plc and building-level plc.	Sept, then monitored Sept to May	Each grade level will develop a SMART Goal aligned with one of the Essentials and DIBELS subtests. Instructional Facilitator will work with grade-level teams/Title staff to ensure DIBELS data is monitored/entered on a weekly basis.	Assessment calendar	Teacher access to DIBELS website, posting data in staff room.
Modify instruction based on assessment results through reflection, planning, small group instruction, and whole group instruction with the aid of an Instructional Facilitator.	Sept to May, Year 1 (2 and 3)	Instructional Facilitator will observe WWW/Reading block and meet at least every other week. Teachers will observe another teacher at least one time per quarter.	Principal will meet with Instructional Facilitator one time per month. Instructional Facilitator will keep track of action plans.	Action Plans, Peer Observation Form.
Develop an afterschool tutoring program (investigate number of days per week, location, length of teacher participation, student participation, funding/budget).	Sept to May, Year 1	Principal discusses with paras, schedule adjustments to ensure personnel from 3:30-4:30 p.m. SI team develops policies/procedures for after-school activities: K-2 Reading Interventions; 3-5 Homework Club, and Reading Interventions.	Monthly update at SI meeting on status of Summer School.	Time during SI team meetings to plan for school year '13-14. Research on effective after-school programs.
Celebrate successful implementation.	Sept to May, and especially December and May	Monthly staff meetings begin with celebration of walkthrough data and sharing of successes from staff members. December and May will have a more formal celebration and sharing at the District level.	Agenda from staff meetings. SI Team will plan.	Time at staff meetings.

Actions	Schedule	Responsibilities	Monitoring	Resources
Year 2:				
Review and revise Learning Goals, Scales, and Tracking graphs. Review strategies for helping students effectively interact with new knowledge and engaging students (Ch. 2 & 5).	Year 1, 2	See Year 1	See Year 1	See Year 1
Helping students practice and deepen their understanding of new knowledge (Ch. 3).	Year 2	Principal overview 1 week before school starts; train staff and meet with grade levels 1xmo. Teachers will work on answering "What will I do to help my students practice and deepen their understanding of new knowledge?" (PLC: Q1). Instructional Facilitator will aid teachers in reflecting and implementing new practices.	Principal will assess new learning through walkthroughs using Marzano's Observational Protocol. Walkthrough data monitored monthly. Track class progress 3xyr.	*The Art and Science of Teaching*. Weekly/bi-weekly grade level meetings.
Communicating high expectations for all students (Ch. 9).	Year 2	Principal overview 1 week before school starts; train staff and meet with grade levels 1xmo. Teachers will work on answering "What will I do to communicate high expectations for all students?" (PLC: Q1). Instructional Facilitator will aid teachers in reflecting and implementing new practices.	Principal will assess new learning through walkthroughs using Marzano's Observational Protocol. Walkthrough data monitored monthly. Track class progress 3xyr.	*The Art and Science of Teaching*. Weekly/bi-weekly grade level meetings.
Compare Year 1,2 data with alignment of concepts, strategies, and resources. If needed, revise alignment of phonics/phonological strategies, concepts, and/or resources by grade level.	Year 1, 2	Principal and Instructional Facilitator will compare Year 1 DIBELS data with Year 2 DIBELS Data.	Three times per year.	Access to DIBELS website, posting data in staff room.
Modify instruction based on assessment results through reflection, planning, small group instruction, and whole group instruction.	Year 1, 2	Instructional Facilitator will observe WWW/Reading block and meet at least every other week. Teachers will observe another teacher at least one time per quarter.	Principal will meet with Instructional Facilitator one time per month. Instructional Facilitator will keep track of action plans.	Action Plans, Peer Observation Form.

CONTINUOUS IMPROVEMENT AND INNOVATION 85

Actions	Schedule	Responsibilities	Monitoring	Resources
Implement the Tutoring program.	Year 2	Principal, teachers, and paras.	DIBELS	Additional supplies as needed.
Celebrate successful implementation.	Sept to May, and especially December and May	Monthly staff meetings begin with celebration of walkthrough data and sharing of successes from staff members. December and May will have a more formal celebration and sharing at the District level.	Agenda from staff meetings. SI Team will plan.	Time at staff meetings.
Year 3:				
Helping students generate and test hypotheses about new knowledge (Ch. 4).	Year 3	Principal overview 1 week before school starts; train staff and meet with grade levels 1xmo. Teachers will work on answering "What will I do to help students generate and test hypotheses about new knowledge?" (PLC: Q1). Instructional Facilitator will aid teachers in reflecting and implementing new practices.	Principal will assess new learning through walkthroughs using Marzano's Observational Protocol. Walkthrough data monitored monthly. Track class progress 3xyr.	*The Art and Science of Teaching.* Weekly/bi-weekly grade level meetings.
Developing effective lesson organized into a cohesive unit (Ch. 10).	Year 3	Principal overview 1 week before school starts; train staff and meet with grade levels 1xmo. Teachers will work on answering "What will I do to develop effective lessons organized into a cohesive unit?" (PLC: Q1). Instructional Facilitator will aid teachers in reflecting and implementing new practices.	Principal will assess new learning through walkthroughs using Marzano's Observational Protocol. Walkthrough data monitored monthly. Track class progress 3xyr.	*The Art and Science of Teaching.* Weekly/bi-weekly grade level meetings.
Compare Year 1, 2, 3 data with alignment of concepts, strategies, and resources. If needed, revise alignment of phonics/phonological strategies, concepts, and/or resources by grade level.	Year 1, 2, 3	Principal and Instructional Facilitator will compare Year 1 and 2 DIBELS data with Year 3 DIBELS data.	Three times per year.	Access to DIBELS website, posting data in staff room.
Modify instruction based on assessment results through reflection, planning, small group, instruction and whole group instruction.	Year 1, 2, 3	Instructional Facilitator will observe WWW/Reading block and meet at least every other week. Teachers will observe another teacher at least one time per quarter.	Principal will meet with Instructional Facilitator one time per month. Instructional Facilitator will keep track of action plans.	Action Plans, Peer Observation Form.

Actions	Schedule	Responsibilities	Monitoring	Resources
Modify tutoring program based on participation and student performance results.	Year 3	SI team works with paras and principal to refine tutoring program.	After-school tutoring program modified as dictated by DIBELS results.	Time to plan during SI meetings.
Celebrate successful implementation.	Sept to May, and especially December and May	Monthly staff meetings begin with celebration of walkthrough data and sharing of successes from staff members. December and May will have a more formal celebration and sharing at the District level.	Agenda from staff meetings. SI Team will plan.	Time at staff meetings.

In order to highlight how this action plan meets the elements of Continuous Improvement and Innovation, let's take each item separately and identify how this plan meets that criteria:

a. Focusing resources on a small number of goals

There is one goal for the school: improving literacy. This goal provides a focus for the school and is a high-leverage area for improving student learning, in general. Additionally, Juan has an overarching plan for creating a language for instruction by way of Marzano's Instructional Framework. Each year, the school is focusing on just a few of the aspects of that framework.

b. Data collection and analysis

Prior to the development of this action plan, the SI Team did a comprehensive look at all of their data—including student demographics and performance, school effectiveness (program and perception data), and school and community contexts (including perception). This resulted in the development of a comprehensive profile of the school—roughly twenty pages in length—that is updated a couple of times during the year as new data becomes available.

Additionally, the plan has the use of ongoing implementation data. This includes walkthrough data, staff implementation of the instructional framework, and student performance data—in this case, DIBELS. In remote learning settings, the shift in implementation data becomes more challenging yet still doable. Walkthroughs, whether as staff observing each other or principal observing teachers, become virtual. Indeed, in a remote learning setting this might even become easier, as teachers are generally not directly supervising students the vast majority of their day. No matter how the data is collected, a concerted effort on ensuring equitable practices is made at all times.

c. The use of multiple sources to guide and demonstrate improvement
In addition to the data from the profile and implementation data, the school has identified specific objectives for improvement. This includes DIBELS and Rigby data with the goal of 90% of students proficient by the end of the three years. This may be one aspect of remote learning that we have yet to master: how to assess students through standardized measures like DIBELS, Rigby, and FastBridge. Hearing students read and using benchmarking tools to assist with this process may be more important than ever.

d. Research-based decision-making
The entire plan is based on research. Marzano's Instructional Framework is well-researched and lays the foundation for innovation—a culture of innovativeness—among the staff.

e. A simple focus on refining processes in small ways
You'll notice that, each year, there is a new focus (from the outset, anyway—it is likely that Year 1 will carry over into Year 2, as the plan is quite ambitious). The focus is small—Engagement Strategies and Monitoring Student Progress. Staff meetings are focused on this work, as well as PLC team meetings. Doing this work remotely still continues.

f. Clear, frequent talk about instruction
The principal is conducting frequent walkthroughs of classrooms and gathering implementation data for the school. Conversations about instruction are part of staff meetings, PLC meetings, discussions with

the Instructional Facilitator, and more. And these conversations and walkthroughs continue in a remote learning environment.

g. Recognition and celebration for superior practices and results
Each month's staff meeting, virtually or in-person, has an element of formal celebration and recognition—both recognizing specific people and celebrating excellent practices. Additionally, more in-depth and formal celebrations occur halfway through the school year and at the end (again, virtually or in-person). Finally, data from the walkthroughs and SMART Goals are posted in the staff meeting room so that regular recognition is part of the daily work of staff—and in remote learning this data can and should be brought up regularly as part of remote meetings. Of course, breaking down data to celebrate equitable practices and ensure closing of gaps is uppermost in their minds.

h. Inventiveness/Innovativeness where risk-taking is encouraged
The context of this action plan has teams of teachers meeting on a weekly basis to implement their learning using the PLC process outlined by the DuFour's. The structure of the plan provides a strategic direction for inventiveness and innovativeness. The monthly staff development meetings encourage this innovativeness through celebration of success. And the conversations that the principal has with staff regarding how individuals are implementing their learning leads to ongoing inventiveness. All of this can and should continue in a virtual setting and is even more important given the circumstances.

i. High expectations for learning
The goal of 90% proficiency is a high goal—especially given the fact that the baseline status of proficiency was around 40%. The attainment of this goal will require the closing of those persistent gaps between groups of students.

j. Using groups as the main units for improvement
Again, the PLC process involves the teaming of staff in grade-level

groupings who meet at least weekly throughout the year. All implementation goes through these Learning Teams—virtually or in-person.

WANTING MORE?

There are a variety of models of continuous improvement. I am a big advocate of choosing one and then following it faithfully. Don't just say that you're doing continuous improvement and then do whatever you want, whenever you want. **Do** continuous improvement.

With the advent of ESSA, it seems that most states have identified continuous improvement processes that schools can adopt and/or adapt. If that's the case for you, that model could very well work. If that's not your situation, here are a few other options to consider.

National Study of School Evaluation. (2006). *Breakthrough School Improvement: An Action Guide for Greater and Faster Results.* Schaumberg, IL: National Study of School Evaluation.

The Breakthrough Model from the National Study of School Evaluation is highly systematic and, together with a companion resource book, provides all of the tools necessary to do school improvement that gets results. The tools sometimes have too much education jargon, but with some study and tweaking, they will produce outstanding results. Additionally, you may have to dig around some old bookshelves to find this book, as it is no longer in print. If you have one, you're in luck: use it! If you don't have (or can't get) a copy, you can use the steps below to assist you in thinking about how to engage in systematic continuous improvement.

The Breakthrough Model is based on four phases of improvement, each with specific Key Actions. The Key Actions then have specific activities in which to engage. The phases and Key Actions are:

Vision
1. Examine research-based factors related to student performance
2. Determine beliefs
3. Develop a shared vision to focus school improvement efforts
4. Determine expectations for student learning

Profile
5. Describe students and their performance
6. Describe school effectiveness
7. Describe the school and community context
8. Determine target areas for improvement

Plan and Implementation
9. Identify gaps between current and expected student performance
10. Set improvement goals
11. Determine interventions
12. Develop action plans
13. Implement, monitor, and adjust interventions

Results
14. Identify measures to determine results
15. Analyze and document student performance results
16. Evaluate the success of interventions
17. Communicate and use results for further improvement

Making Schools Work: School and Classroom Practices that Prepare Students for College and Careers (https://www.sreb.org/post/making-schools-work)

"SREB's **Making Schools Work** school improvement process uses a distributed leadership approach to involve the whole school in identifying problems of practice that impact student engagement and achievement and developing plans to solve them."

Using specific designs for elementary, middle, and high school and technology centers, Making Schools Work "empowers school teams to create improvement plans that address five focus areas." Regarding continuous improvement, specifically, they have a "problem-solving process [that] draws on engineering design principles to support focus teams as they determine actions to take to foster supportive learning environments, integrate academic and technical content, improve student achievement and empower youth to explore and achieve their career goals."

Baldrige in Education (http://www.nist.gov/baldrige/)

The Baldrige Performance Excellence Framework is a comprehensive framework used in business/industry, education, and healthcare. Complete with a plethora of tools, resources, and self-assessments, Baldrige also has an annual presidential award for which schools can apply to demonstrate that they are meeting the criteria.

Self-Assess and Apply Your Knowledge

Use the following table to self-assess your knowledge on each of the statements. Note how you go about bridging any knowing-doing gap in order to make each one a reality.

	I need to learn more	I know this	I can teach others	What I DO to make this happen
Focus resources on a small number of goals				
Data collection and analysis				
The use of multiple information sources to guide and demonstrate improvement				
Research-based decision-making				
A simple focus on refining processes in small ways				
Clear, frequent talk about teaching				
Clear, frequent talk about learning				
Recognition and celebration for superior practices and results				
Inventiveness/Innovativeness and Risk-taking on the part of teachers				
High expectations for student learning				
Using groups of teachers as the main way for improving student learning				

CHAPTER SIX

Model Learning

Elements of Principal Knowledge in Creating a Collaborative Workplace Environment for Teachers

To build a collaborative culture of professional learning, principals know and understand that they must:

6. Model professional learning by participating in administrator learning communities
    A. Default mode: Learning
    B. Leadership vs. Management

Quality leadership is not simply about giving directives but about seeking answers and asking questions. As Lambert (1998, p. 9) noted, "Leadership is about learning that leads to constructive change." There is no silver bullet, no easy answers. Principals must be ready and willing to learn.

Default Mode: Learning

Heifetz noted that leadership is about facilitating learning and seeking out adaptive solutions to adaptive problems. This requires humility in one's approach, and a constant striving to improve. And these attitudes of learning and humility, coupled with the skills necessary to convey these, are foundational to leadership that engenders constructive change.

Though there might be times that directives are necessary, the default leadership mode should be one of learning. For example, a bomb threat is not a time for learning from each other about possible options for moving kids to a safe environment, contacting the authorities, and coordinating staff. Instead, situations like this require someone to take charge and make decisions based on collaborative pre-planning—and this falls to the designated leadershipto the designated leadership; directives are absolutely necessary.

In the day-to-day operations of running a school, where acute life or death emergencies are the exception rather than the rule, a posture of learning is critical to effective leadership. As noted earlier, in conducting staff meetings, the focus should be on learning. In reflecting on current practice, the center of attention should be on improvement. In considering changes to instruction, adult learning should be central.

Leadership vs. Management

Deming, the founder of TQM—Total Quality Management—notes that the key difference between leadership and management is how the leader responds to needs. Fundamentally, leadership is about finding and meeting the needs of everyone, whereas management is about accommodating the unique individual needs of each person. Though both are necessary, past education systems tended to place their focus on managing schools—smooth bus operations, substitute placement, student and staff discipline, etc. Management, then, focuses on those specific aspects of the organization that tend toward individual issues.

On the other hand, leadership, according to Deming, is more about finding and meeting the needs of everyone in the system; leadership is about working on the system. The organization itself must be modified through continuous improvement, and this is where leadership is distinguished from management. When leadership is about learning, it is also about meeting the professional needs of everyone in the system. To put it another way, leadership is working *on* the system. Management is working *in* the system.

Another example of the importance of learning comes from Barth. He shares a story of disengaged employees and how leaders must re-engage these employees by asking themselves, essentially, "What conditions can I devise that will bring this person back to life as a learner?" He contends that leaders must be inventive and persistent and hold high expectations in order to answer this question. The result is "membership in good standing of a Professional *Learning* Community" (emphasis added, Barth, 2005, p.

123). Again, the link between leadership and learning is emphasized.

The National Association of Elementary School Principals identified a number of standards to which principals must strive in order to be effective. In regard to creating a culture of adult learning (Standard 1), this standard includes an element focused on your own learning as a principal. A principal engaged in creating a culture of adult learning will be committed to increasing knowledge, skills, and capacities through professional development, peer mentoring and the establishment and support of schoolwide learning communities. A previous version of the standards stated that principals "recognize the need to continually improve [the] principals' own professional practice" (NAESP, 2002, p. 42).

What this means is that, in order to create a collaborative environment for teachers, a principal must model adult learning by engaging in practices similar to teachers but with colleagues from settings similar to their own. Participate with other administrators in one or more learning communities to model continuous improvement and professional learning and to become a more effective instructional leader. Don't just talk about professional learning. *Do* the professional learning. As you engage in professional learning, especially focused on learning by doing, virtually and/or in-person, you will become even better.

Modeling Professional Learning in Practice (including Remotely)

Before beginning, please note that this entire vignette is equally applicable in face-to-face and virtual settings. As you read, consider the implications in both scenarios.

Natalia is a high school principal in a suburban community. Once a week she meets with her administrative team consisting of three assistant principals and the activity director. To emphasize the importance of her own, and their, learning, they begin each meeting with roughly thirty minutes of professional learning. These thirty minutes are held sacred, and they almost never skip this portion to deal with other management issues.

When Natalia first began this practice of emphasizing the professional learning of her administrative team, some of the others balked. One, in particular, vocally disapproved of the practice. But Natalia persisted and drew this individual into a leadership role among the administrative team. Each week, one person was assigned to lead the next week's professional learning. By doing this, Natalia was able to gradually win over all of the administrators into seeing how important their professional learning was to improving the school.

Once per month, Natalia and the leadership team assign themselves to read a professional journal article on leadership—depending on the current emphasis of the School Improvement Team and what they are experiencing in the school. Another meeting per month begins with an emphasis on the application of what they are learning. For example, when they are studying walkthrough types and developing their own form for use, they bring evidence of having completed walkthroughs. They discuss the feedback provided to teachers, and critique each other to provide additional feedback.

Typically, the protocol that will be emphasized with staff at the next staff meeting is tried out amongst themselves. Natalia always wants to see how the protocol will *actually* work. Additionally, she wants to experience what the teachers will experience. And she wants to be able to make revisions to the protocol before going to the entire staff.

This leaves two remaining meetings per month. The focus for these is on examining the products that the PLC teams in the building are completing. For example, teams turn in sample assessments and the student performance data associated with those assessments. At their weekly meeting, the administrative team looks at the same data as the teachers and comes to their own conclusions. They then examine the work of the teachers and discuss specific feedback that needs to be provided to teams to advance the teacher's work. Finally, at least once per month, the meeting begins by conducting classroom walkthroughs as a team and debriefing what they see throughout the school in the implementation of best practices of the school improvement action plan.

Additionally, Natalia meets monthly with District-level administrators and principals from other buildings to engage in similar learning. They hold themselves accountable to each other for implementing the learning about assessments, data usage, and instructional strategies. Each meeting includes bringing copies of agendas from building-level meetings, as well as products of staff learning (assessments, student performance results, etc). Natalia makes sure to bring this learning back to her assistant principals and activity director for application in their school.

Natalia also goes to learning opportunities outside of the building and outside of the sphere of administrators. When teachers go to a training—no matter the content area—she tries to have one of the administrators attend with them. Because of this, the trainings that teachers attend are focused and deliberate—and there are almost always a number of teachers (with an administrator) who attend. Rarely do one or two teachers go to disconnected or episodic trainings by themselves.

In addition to these formal meetings, the building principals use language conducive to learning. Natalia frequently uses phrases such as "One of the strategies we're learning about is…" or "Something you might consider is…" or "Some of our colleagues learned about…." This language is in stark contrast to, "This is a strategy you need to use…" or "Do this…."

WANTING MORE?

Association of Supervision and Curriculum Development
  www.ascd.org
Learning Forward
  www.learningforward.org
Phi Delta Kappa
  www.pdkintl.org

National Association of Elementary School Principals
www.naesp.org
National Association of Secondary School Principals
www.nassp.org

As you know, professional organizations are an excellent source of professional learning materials. And because of the explosion of the web, numerous articles can be obtained online. Simple Google searches, or searches within each organization, will typically yield a plethora of excellent articles and other resources for study. Using the websites will ensure the most recent thinking on topics, as well as, typically, short summaries that are perfect for a thirty-minute discussion for the leadership team.

Self-Assess and Apply Your Knowledge

Use the following table to self-assess your knowledge on each of the statements. Note how you go about bridging any knowing-doing gap in order to make each one a reality.

	I need to learn more	I know this	I can teach others	What I DO to make this happen
Learn alongside my staff				
Learn from a mentor				
Plan together with other principals about professional issues				
Think together with other principals				
Observe and respond to teaching with other principals				
Observe and respond to assessment with other principals				
Focus on improving instruction with other principals				
Use protocols (step-by-step procedures for teams) with other principals				

CHAPTER SEVEN
Allocate Resources

Elements of Principal Knowledge in Creating a Collaborative Workplace Environment for Teachers

To build a collaborative culture of professional learning, principals know and understand that:

7. Resources should be allocated to improve student learning
   A. Tangible resources
      1. Time
      2. Materials
      3. Equipment
      4. Space
   B. Intangible resources
      1. Training on protocols and procedures
      2. Administrative support
      3. Trust between teachers
      4. Access to new ideas and expertise

Creating a collaborative culture of professional learning doesn't just happen because someone simply wants it to happen. Resources are necessary. And these resources include time, materials, equipment, space, training on protocols and procedures, administrative support, trust between teachers, and access to new ideas and expertise. Let's deal with each of these separately, after first surveying the literature on what resources are necessary and why they are important—especially since some of these resources aren't what necessarily first come to mind when saying the word "resources."

Necessary Resources

Learning Forward (NSDC, 2003, p. 69) identified a number of required "resources to support adult learning and collaboration." While it is somewhat dated, the clarity of their list is most appreciated in that the principal:

- Allocates resources to support job-embedded professional development in the school
- Focuses resources on a small number of high-priority goals
- Allocates resources to provide for continuous improvement of school staff
- Allocates resources so technology supports student learning

"Resources" is also among the identified twenty-one leadership responsibilities (Marzano et al., 2005) that have the greatest impact on student learning. In that seminal study, resources were defined as "the alignment of several levels of resources necessary to analyze, plan, and take action in response to opportunities and threats that the future brings" (Deering, Dilts & Russell, 2003, p. 34).

Given that Learning Forward and Marzano et al. say that resources are important, what are those resources? Fullan (2020) states that instructional improvement requires resources in the form of materials, equipment, space, time, and access to new ideas and to expertise. Note that the responsibility of leaders in providing resources goes beyond equipment and supplies. It includes "space, time, and access to new ideas and expertise" among the necessary ingredients for creating an environment where collaboration for improvement of student learning is the norm.

In addition to the fairly tangible resources noted by Fullan, other researchers note more intangible resources that are necessary to create a collaborative workplace environment for teachers. These include training on protocols and procedures, administrative support, and trust between teachers (NSDC, 2003).

At the risk of belaboring this point, the National Association of Elementary School Principals states that principals engaged in creating a culture of adult learning will:

1. Provide time for reflection as an important part of improving practice
2. Invest in teacher learning
3. Connect professional development to school learning goals
4. Provide opportunities for teachers to work, plan, and think together
5. Recognize the need to continually improve principals' own professional practice. (NAESP, 2002, p. 42)

Specific Resources

Having shared a broad look at what resources are needed to create a collaborative environment for teachers, let's now take a closer look. Resources can be thought of as being in two categories, as implied above: 1) Tangible Resources and 2) Intangible Resources. Tangible Resources are those that are concrete and tend to be comparatively easy to allocate: Time, Materials, Equipment, and Space. On the other hand, Intangible Resources are comparatively more difficult to develop and rely on human interactions: Training on protocols and procedures, Administrative support, Trust between teachers, and Access to new ideas and expertise.

TANGIBLE RESOURCES: Time, Materials, Equipment, and Space

Tangible resources are, in some ways, straightforward and easy to understand. Principals must invest in teacher learning by providing tangible resources for educators to work, plan, and think together. If this is not provided for collaboration, the likelihood of it naturally arising is low.

> This free download can be quite helpful in examining the use of time in our schools, and in considering ways to carve out this resource for professional learning. https://learningforward.org/wp-content/uploads/2017/09/establishing-time-for-professional-learning.pdf

Materials requested by staff that are in line with School Improvement priorities must be provided to further professional learning. These materials might include books to engage in the study of assessment literacy or instructional best practices, or access to internet resources, or journal articles on timely topics.

At the root of providing materials for professional learning is the need for the principal to know what materials to recommend. To do this, the principal must stay abreast of current research, or connect themselves to others who are connected to the research. The district office can be a key resource, as well as intermediate service agencies. Institutions of higher education are also typically excellent resources, as are professional organizations.

Not only must materials requested by teachers be provided, but designated leadership must engage staff in pushing them toward higher levels of learning and application. For example, a district working to improve student engagement needs to provide materials to staff on what engagement looks like. If staff are to use response cards with students as a means to engage them in responding to queries during instruction, then materials for the development of response cards must be provided. If principals want staff to clearly understand how engagement looks in the classroom, then video examples and/or learning walks of best practice must be utilized. The building principal and leadership team must be thinking ahead and anticipating potential materials that staff may need to implement expected practices.

Equipment is also a tangible resource that is necessary to create a collaborative culture for professional learning. This may include technology resources for the creation of high-quality assessments, rubrics, checklists, etc. It may also include access to a photocopier to duplicate these same high-quality tools. Further, equipment like an ELMO or document camera with LCD projector may benefit the actual collaboration time. A specific example of the use of this equipment may be the examination of student work whereby teachers can all see the student's work projected while a specific protocol is used to examine that work.

Finally, space must be provided to staff in order to create a collaborative workplace environment. It may seem quite simple, and it is: If teachers do not have a physical (or virtual) space in which to meet on a regular basis to collaborate, then they won't—and maybe even can't—collaborate effectively. They need space: a physical teacher's room will do just fine (as long as it is a non-distracting space), or a virtual room through digital technology.

One final note on tangible resources, and that is that all of these can be provided with little or no additional costs. Many materials requested from staff can be made by hand, or photocopied, or accessed from a website, or developed with a basic Word or Excel file, or purchased with a very small amount of funds—of which federal Title IIA dollars is an excellent resource (and reason to be sure to advocate for this resource from your elected representatives). Regarding space, I've seen many schools, almost all of which were limited in space, find ways to create room for teachers to work. Finally, equipment like document cameras and LCD projectors are tools that can and should be used in classrooms and with staff learning. So it really should not require additional fiscal resources—but just a borrowing or re-purposing of the equipment when not being used for instruction.

INTANGIBLE RESOURCES: Training on protocols and procedures, administrative support, trust between teachers, and access to new ideas and expertise

Intangible Resources are much more complex than time, materials, equipment, and space. However, without these intangible resources, you will have very little or no success at all in creating a collaborative workplace environment for teachers.

Putting the "C" in PLC involves the development of trust between teachers. Cultures of low trust tend to be high anxiety—and high anxiety runs counter to collaboration. High trust cultures build momentum and allow collaboration to flourish. To build this trust, protocols are essential.

In a *New York Times Magazine* article, "What Google Learned From Its Quest to Build the Perfect Team," Charles Duhigg (2016) summarized a multi-year study of some 180 teams at Google and found one thing above all else impacted the effectiveness of the group. This one thing wasn't the education of the individuals, the personalities of those same individuals, how well they got along as a team, or any other factor attributed to what people typically think about in terms of individual or group dynamics. Instead, the one thing that made the difference between effective and less-than-effective teams was psychological safety.

Further, this psychological safety was based on group norms in which individuals set aside their personal proclivities during group work and honored team norms. Two essential attributes came to the forefront: 1) Equity of turn-taking and 2) Social sensitivity (or the ability to tell how others feel based on their tone of voice, their expressions, and other nonverbal cues). It was these two characteristics that were vital in creating an effective team and a climate of interpersonal trust and mutual respect that foster task success.

While social sensitivity is harder to develop in others, equity of turn-taking need not be so: this is where protocols come in handy, as this is precisely what protocols do. Simply put, protocols are a step-by-step process for doing something. The purpose of a protocol is to focus a group on a specific task and to provide for equitable opportunities for expressing one's thinking.

Staff need to be trained on protocols to maximize their effectiveness—otherwise people default into their natural tendencies of interrupting, dominating, or sitting passively while others do the dominating. Protocols for examining student work and data analysis are particularly useful for educators. Some of the most popular protocols are the Tuning

Protocol and the Last Word Protocol. A simple Google search on the internet will turn up a number of protocols that can be helpful in a variety of situations.

> An incredible, detailed listing of dozens of protocols is available for free online from the School Reform Initiative: (https://www.schoolreforminitiative.org/protocols/). Do your own searches online, as well, and you'll find a plethora of excellent protocols for just about any situation.

Procedures are also important to create a collaborative workplace environment for teachers—just as they are important for students in a classroom. What procedures do you have in place for staff to document implementation of their professional learning? What about procedures for turning in notes of team meetings? Do you have procedures for signing in/documenting attendance at sessions? There are numerous procedures that can and should be put into place to facilitate professional learning of staff.

Administrative support is also a key resource for the effectiveness of creating a collaborative workplace environment for teachers, and there are many ways that a principal can signal administrative support. Not only does this imply social and emotional support from administrative staff in the development of a high-performing collaborative culture, but it also involves support in other ways.

Administrative support may include a rearranging of staff meetings to become focused on staff learning and not management issues of the school (see Chapter Three for a fuller discussion). I understand that principals also have to manage their schools. But this needs to be done in other ways. As one young principal once told me as he worked to focus staff meetings on staff learning, "I put all of my adminis-trivia into a memo—which took me more time—but it made the meeting so much more productive! We were able to truly focus on improving our practice to improve student learning." A sample memo to staff, outlining adminis-trivia, is provided in Chapter Three.

Administrative support may also include the reduction or even elimination of certain bureaucratic activities in which teachers are frequently required to engage so that they may focus their energies on improving student learning. Maybe copies of detailed lesson plans are minimized. Maybe paperwork to request professional leave is reduced. No doubt you will identify places to reduce bureaucracy in your building if you take some time to think about it—or, even better, ask your staff for their ideas on what they spend significant time doing that has a minimal or no impact on student learning.

You are right to believe that this will be a welcome relief to many teachers—but be ready. My experience is that some teachers will cling to these time-wasters and will explain to you why they are absolutely vital to student learning. You will need to make a decision to either, 1) stay firm, 2) wean them off slowly, or 3) decide to deal with the reduction of some adminis-trivia later. At some point, though, you will need to make this happen in order to build a truly collaborative culture dedicated to improving educator effectiveness and results for students.

The final intangible resource is that of providing access to new ideas and expertise to teaching staff. I personally like to think of these as "instructional hand grenades" in the professional learning process. As teams work, outside expertise will be vital.

As Fullan (2003) puts it, groups can be powerful. They can also be powerfully wrong! Hence, it is important to loft strategic and specific instructional grenades into the professional learning of staff. This can be in the form of video or other conferences, webinars, book studies, outside experts on training days, workshops, and more.

As noted earlier, "one of the most frequently mentioned resources important to the effective functioning of a school is the professional development opportunities for teachers" (Marzano et al., 2005, p. 59). Remember, too, that Schmoker clarifies that traditional professional development is overrated: the most effective form of professional learning is teachers working in teams for the improvement of student learning. The focus of professional learning is on the team, and periodic instructional grenades are important resources for creating a collaborative workplace environment for teachers.

Allocating Resources in Practice (including Remotely)

Karyn is an elementary building principal of a four-section school. She has arranged the master schedule so that teachers have thirty minutes of daily, uninterrupted planning time with their grade-level peers and special education teacher. One day per week the team focuses on logistics of upcoming field trips, special events, and other managerial-type activities. Another day per week is reserved for a focus on students—dealing with social, emotional, behavioral, or other issues to ensure the success of specific students with individual difficulties. The other three days per week are focused on professional learning that improves student learning.

Karyn structured these days at the very beginning of the year by allowing teams to choose which day of the week they will primarily focus on which tasks (knowing that some flexibility may be necessary, depending on circumstances). Karyn emphasized that three days per week *must* be spent on collaborative inquiry into improving their professional practice. In order to monitor these guidelines, Karyn asked for notes from team meetings to be submitted electronically to her. Specific work-products are expected from teams—such as common assessments, charts of data from those common assessments, jointly developed lesson plans, examples of student work measured against common rubrics, etc.

Karyn ensured that a physical room in the building was dedicated to collaborative teams—whether that be one of the teacher's classrooms or another room. She guarantees the availability of equipment in this space—including an LCD projector, an ELMO/document camera, tables, and chairs.

To start the year, Karyn employed a number of "get to know

you" activities to build trust in each grade-level team. Included among these was the development of norms, the naming of each team, and some purely fun activities. She modeled a data analysis protocol with all staff so that they could see the protocol in action. At the first staff meeting, once staff had a chance to compile some data, she again walked staff through the protocol, allowing them to engage in guided practice to ensure appropriate use of the protocol. She followed up in the next week's team meeting to see that teams were using the protocol in that setting, and then again later in the month. She also worked to make sure that data was being looked at in such a way as to identify inequities and then address these as close to the issue as possible.

At the beginning of the year, too, Karyn provided all staff with a three-ring notebook with section dividers to hold materials for the course of the year. Included in this binder were forms for feedback to the principal after each team meeting, protocols to assist with the work, examples of common assessments that prior-year teachers had used, and other materials necessary for the creation of a collaborative workplace environment for the teachers. Some tabs in the binder were pre-labeled (Norms, Feedback Forms, Assessments, Data, Protocols), and others were left blank for teachers to use as they needed.

Karyn preferred using a physical binder because this became a tangible item that was taken to meetings and used throughout the year, as opposed to a digital binder that some were better at using than others. However, as the year got going, there were some teams who took the materials and created their own Google drives or folders with the same documents. Depending on the team, this worked well. Some teams, however, preferred to use the hard-copy materials, and Karyn was more than happy with this arrangement. One staff member had even mentioned creating a Google Classroom for the staff, as "students" of the class run by the principal, to access, use, and turn in their work products, and this was something that Karyn was considering for the future. However, Karyn didn't want the inability of some staff to be as fluent with technology to get in the way of creating a collaborative environment, so she was thoughtful about how she might move forward with this.

Finally, once per month, at the building staff meetings, Karyn and the School Improvement Team provided just-in-time professional learning for the staff. In September, they noticed that staff were having trouble analyzing their DIBELS data and translating the results into practice, especially thinking about subgroups of students and specific students to close gaps. So Karyn worked with the District office and another building in the District to provide specific training to her staff during the meeting.

The teaching staff appreciated the focus of Karyn on improving student learning. They liked having a notebook to keep all of their materials. They felt heard and supported because of the just-in-time learning at staff meetings. They understood how the work of school improvement was aligned with their practices, and how their practices were supporting school improvement. They felt valued, respected, and professional.

In October, it became apparent through classroom walk-through data that staff were struggling with maintaining engagement of students. So Karyn accessed the expertise of certain staff, videotaped excellent lessons using specific engagement strategies, and shared these clips at the building staff meeting. The meeting included opportunities for staff themselves to engage in the strategies, as well as time to plan when and where they would use the strategies in upcoming lessons.

Finally, Karyn attended at least one of the weekly collaborative planning time meetings per week for at least a portion of the meeting. She wanted staff to know, in word and in deed, that she supported their work. Additionally, she highlighted specific teams' accomplishments in her weekly update to all staff in the building. And, last but not least, she wrote handwritten notes to specific teams and teachers emphasizing excellence. By mid-September she made sure that every staff member had received a note, and continued throughout the year to send at least one note per quarter to every teacher.

With the exception of providing a physical space for meetings and having hard-copy binders for materials, everything done by Karyn is completely possible in a remote learning environment. Regarding having a physical space, in a remote setting teachers need access to and an understanding of how to use tools for their facilitation (e.g., Zoom, GoogleMeet, Microsoft Teams, etc). And the hard-copy binders for materials may still be useful for each member, though I suspect that the digital push coming from COVID-19 will supersede this, and the move to Google Classroom will happen sooner rather than later.

Self-Assess and Apply Your Knowledge

Use the following table to self-assess your knowledge on each of the statements. Note how you go about bridging any knowing-doing gap in order to make each one a reality.

	I need to learn more	I **know** this	I can teach others	What I DO to make this happen
Allocate time				
Provide materials				
Provide equipment				
Ensure space				
Provide training in the use of protocols (step-by-step procedures for teams)				
Provide administrative support				
Create conditions for trust between teachers				
Provide Access to new ideas				
Provide Access to expertise				

CHAPTER EIGHT

Involve Staff

> **Elements of Principal Knowledge in Creating a Collaborative Workplace Environment for Teachers**
>
> **To build a collaborative culture of professional learning, principals know and understand that:**
>
> 8. **Staff should be involved in important decisions**
>   A. The use of a leadership team
>   B. Opportunity for input is provided, encouraged, expected, implemented

Leadership matters.

The principal is the most important leader because they can empower their staff or tie their hands. The principal can either trust their staff to do their job or micromanage them. Micromanaging takes up valuable time. It keeps principals from getting to the really important (and fun!) work of school improvement.

Even though the principal is the most important leader in the school, leadership is not just the work of those in *designated* leadership positions. Designated leadership (i.e., the principal) creates the conditions and environment for a collaborative culture. They do this by building the leadership capacity of all individuals within the organization. Designated leadership sets the tone, establishes the direction, and creates the culture within the school.

Building Leadership Capacity

Building leadership capacity does not mean that the principal gives away all of the leadership. You don't and can't walk away from your responsibilities. Rather, the principal has to be aware, be involved, see the bigger picture, and provide insight to leadership teams. And the principal must be trusted by the staff.

So what is needed to build leadership capacity?

One of the longest-standing and more consistent philosophies of school reform is Larry Lezotte's (2005) "Correlates of Effective Schools," now in their second generation and fifth decade. The first correlate identified by Lezotte is Instructional Leadership, and a key aspect of this is the need for a core leadership group. The responsibility of this group is "to initiate and sustain an ongoing conversation of school change based on the Effective Schools research" (Lezotte, 2005, p. 183), where opportunities for input from all staff are provided, encouraged, expected, and implemented. This is because the use of a core leadership group builds capacity and strengthens ownership in improvement initiatives.

As a structure for thinking about leadership, Lambert (1998) identified five basic tenets that I think are still quite useful more than two decades later. These tenets provide a context for the involvement of staff in decision-making. Though I am listing all five for your reference, four of these tenets are specifically applicable to this particular element of principal knowledge.

1. Leadership is not trait theory; leadership and leader are not the same.
2. Leadership is about learning that leads to constructive change.
3. Everyone has the potential and right to work as a leader.
4. Leading is a shared endeavor.
5. Leadership requires the redistribution of power and authority. (Lambert, 1998, pp. 8–9)

Leadership ≠ Leader

Leadership does not depend on those sitting in the office of the principal, confined to one person. "Leadership and leader are not the same" means that leadership emerges from different individuals based on the situations in which they are placed. Known as distributed leadership, the contention is that if one does not design appropriate avenues for leadership to emerge, it will emerge on its own, in unwanted, unsolicited, and negative ways.

An example of leadership distributing itself might be expressed as grievances to the local education association. If designated leaders do not appropriately address and/or accommodate grievances, these grievances might result in negotiation problems. Ultimately, the issue might even lead to a labor strike in some states.

In the end, power always becomes distributed. It is up to designated leadership to proactively and appropriately distribute that power. Otherwise, it will distribute itself in what might be destructive and inappropriate ways.

But distributing leadership is not just about avoiding negative consequences. It also leads to positive results. Proactively distributing leadership leads to greater staff ownership in decisions. And greater staff ownership leads to higher levels of implementation. And higher levels of implementation lead to improved student learning.

> Distributing leadership leads to greater staff ownership in decisions.
> Greater staff ownership in decisions leads to higher level of implementation.
> Higher levels of implementation lead to improved student learning.

In terms of creating a collaborative environment, the idea that leader and leadership are not the same means that all instructional staff must be involved in the work of leadership. Since leadership and leader are not the same, leadership cannot wait for one person to arise to serve in the capacity of leader: the work of leadership is the responsibility and right of every staff member. So a key focus of creating a collaborative environment must be the development of leadership skills and capacity in the entire staff.

Potential and Right of Leadership

"Everyone has the potential and right to work as a leader" broadens the scope and provides for unlimited potential. This third tenet from Lambert speaks to the reality that there are no limits to who can lead and in what capacity; on the contrary, everyone will arise to lead at different times.

There are two critical assumptions in this statement: (a) that staff have the capacity to work as leaders, and (b) they are entitled to the work of leadership. This is a quantum shift in previous thinking, as it has typically been thought that only certain folks lead, and the rest follow. According to DePree (1989, p. 24), "Everyone has the right and the duty to influence decision making and to understand the results."

A principal must then know where to involve staff in developing school policies and in providing input to important decisions. Further, those opportunities for staff involvement must not only be provided, but encouraged and expected. Finally, a core leadership team must be empowered to make and implement decisions.

One final note on the implementation of decisions made by the core leadership team: implementation is critical. When principals decide to pull a group together—such as a core leadership team—that group must be empowered to make decisions. Part of that empowerment is the principal ensuring follow-through on decisions. Otherwise, staff will very quickly perceive their time to be wasted. This will lead to a perception that all future work to engage staff in decision-making is a guise for administrative top-down tyranny. And this is antithetical to a collaborative environment.

As an example, a district with which I am familiar was engaged in a textbook adoption process. As part of this process, two different companies (Series A and Series B) were selected to pilot their materials for potential adoption. At the conclusion of the year-long pilot, the recommendation from staff was to adopt Series A. However, the District Office staff decided that neither Series A nor Series B was appropriate for purchase. Series C was purchased.

More than five years later, many staff were still resentful of the District Office decision. Despite turnover of staff at the District level, distrust still reigned. New personnel continued to battle the lack of trust, and ownership in the use of Series C was low. It was never implemented with fidelity, and there were literally efforts to undermine its use. To be blunt, the use of a core leadership team to make the selection of textbook materials was a guise. The result was long-term damage to improving student learning.

Use your core leadership team to make decisions. Then implement those decisions, even if it is not your first choice. If you want input but will be making the final decision as the principal, then let everyone know this is the case—before input is given.

Leadership: A Shared Endeavor Requiring Power and Authority Redistribution

The fourth and fifth tenets of Lambert can be thought of as a simple phrase: the masses are now in charge. This distribution of power and authority happens either through formal channels or unsolicited venues (e.g., the example regarding the distribution of power enunciated for the first tenet where power becomes inappropriately distributed to the local education association).

You must purposefully distribute power so that leadership emerges in productive ways, and you need to know how to distribute leadership and have the repertoire of skills for doing so. You must use structures, systems, and processes (Chapters Two and Three, as well as later in this chapter) to distribute the work of leadership throughout the staff, and then successfully implement those structures, systems, and processes.

Input

The researchers Marzano, Waters, and McNulty (2005) of Mid-continent Research for Education and Learning conducted a meta-analysis of studies on the impact of leadership on student achievement. Their work, published under the title *School Leadership that Works: From Research to Results*, forms a significant milestone clarifying the roles played by school leaders in impacting student learning. The result was twenty-one principal behaviors associated with significant gains in student achievement.

"Input" is one of the principal behaviors identified by Marzano et al. (2005, p. 51), or "the extent to which the school leader involves teachers in the design and implementation of important decisions and policies." Specific skills that principals have in applying input include:

- providing opportunities for staff to be involved in developing school policies,
- providing opportunities for staff input on all important decisions, and
- using leadership teams in decision-making.

A Plan for Staff Involvement

Marzano et al. (2005, p. 98) propose a five-step plan for effective school leadership: "1) Develop a strong school leadership team. 2) Distribute some responsibilities throughout the leadership team. 3) Select the right work. 4) Identify the order of magnitude implied by the selected work. 5) Match the management style to the order of magnitude of the change initiative."

---

1. Develop a strong school leadership team.
2. Distribute some responsibilities throughout the leadership team.
3. Select the right work.
4. Identify the order of magnitude implied by the selected work.
5. Match the management style to the order of magnitude of the change initiative.

The first two steps of this effective school leadership plan involve the development and use of a school leadership team. Principals must create experiences for teachers to serve as instructional leaders within the school by teaming appropriately. Additionally, a principal needs to involve the faculty in planning and implementing high-quality professional learning for the school.

Selecting the Right Work

Marzano et al. (2005) state that the principal must select the right work, then identify the order of magnitude implied by this work. To assist with clarifying exactly what this means, I think Covey (1990) puts it nicely by discussing the difference between "urgent" and "important." Urgent activities are those that must be dealt with immediately. These are potential crises or problems that must be handled right away, but they can also include telephone calls, emails, or meetings of some kind. Urgent issues must be dealt with now, first—but they may or may not be considered important.

A medical analogy might prove useful in considering the difference between important and urgent activities. Urgent activities are those in which a life-threatening situation must be avoided: bypass surgery, removal of cancerous tumors, or other major procedures necessary to save one's life. These are actions undertaken due to an emergency health occurrence. They are urgent.

Important activities, on the other hand, are those that typically have to do with getting results—particularly in the long run. If an activity is considered important, it is probably one that you feel contributes significantly to your personal sense of mission or purpose. And it probably also lends itself to getting the work of your organization's mission accomplished. But an important activity may or may not be considered urgent.

In the medical analogy begun above, important activities are those that maintain and improve health. For instance, eating healthy, exercising, and regular medical check-ups would be among important activities in which one must engage. These contribute to long-term health and are important, but usually none of them are urgent, or an emergency, in terms of saving one's life.

Chart Four provides examples of what might be considered urgent and important activities. The Time Management Matrix juxtaposes these two considerations against each other. By doing this, four quadrants are created.

CHART 4
The Time Management Matrix

	Urgent	Not Urgent

Important	I
	Activities:
	  Crises
	  Pressing problems
	  Deadline-driven projects
		II
		Activities:
		  Prevention
		  Relationship building
		  Recognize new opportunities
		  Planning, recreation

Not Important	III
	Activities:
	  Interruptions, some calls
	  Some mail, some reports
	  Some meetings
	  Proximate, pressing matters
	  Popular activities
		IV
		Activities:
		  Trivia, busywork
		  Some mail
		  Some phone calls
		  Time wasters
		  Pleasant activities

Source: Covey, 1990

Having examined the Covey framework, it is important for the principal to designate to what level of work the School Improvement Team will engage. Those activities in Quadrants I and II are specifically those in which the School Improvement Team should place the majority of its emphasis and energy—especially Quadrant II.

Models of Implementation

Developing a school leadership team can take many forms. One popular form is the use of a School Improvement Leadership Team. By funneling initiatives through a School Improvement process, the building principal can gain coherence. So what might this look like?

To begin, please note that the diagram is specifically non-hierarchical: multiple levels of engagement are available to all staff where no individual is elevated above any others. With the exception of one caveat: clearly

INVOLVE STAFF 119

CHART 5

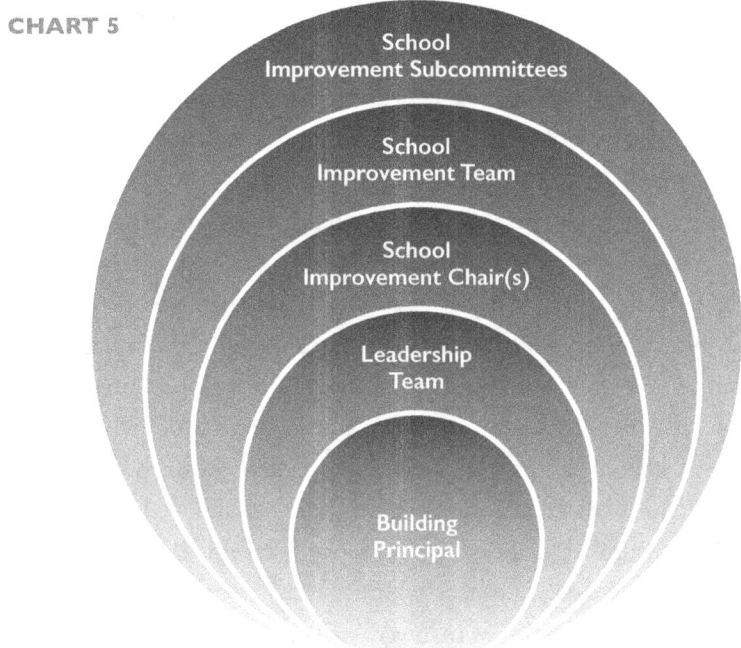

the building principal has the prerogative to be the designated leader in the building. Ultimately, they are responsible for the functioning of the building. In a certain sense, they always reserve veto authority over decisions—though it is wise to exercise this authority very rarely in School Improvement initiatives. Otherwise, you risk undermining the team and wasting everyone's time.

Surrounding the building principal is the larger leadership team: consisting of assistant principal(s), coordinators, instructional coaches, or other designated leaders in the building. Frequently, these individuals can be overlooked in School Improvement—they may be seen as disciplinarians in charge of student behavior and little else. However, it would be wise to include all administrative or quasi-administrative staff, even if on a limited basis, in School Improvement decision-making and implementation.

The first level of inclusion of all teaching staff is at the level of School Improvement Leadership—whether as a chairperson or in the use of multiple chairs. In this regard, my preference is to have at least co-chairs to further distribute leadership. This has the added benefit of likely ensuring continuity through staff turnover. These individuals are critical to the dissemination of information throughout staff and the collection of input from all staff.

In addition to School Improvement Chairs, there needs to be a larger team at the building. This may include so-called department heads, grade-level leaders, or chairs of subcommittees that feed into School Improvement initiatives. The size of the team will vary depending on the number of staff in your building, so be sure to consider membership based on ensuring representation from a cross-section of your building. And the inclusion of non-certified staff will depend on how non-certified staff are involved in instruction in your building. Regardless of the methods, number of people, or composition, this larger committee allows for more widespread feedback into decision-making.

Finally, all staff should be involved, at some level, in subcommittee work of the School Improvement Team. This may be ad-hoc committees for specific periods of time, or long-term standing committees. In any case, the work must be meaningful, allow for and encourage input on decision-making, and at some level involve all staff.

Staff Involvement in Practice (including Remotely)

Jai is the principal of a midsize grade nine through twelve comprehensive high school. Her two assistant principals and one activity director meet weekly to discuss both management and leadership issues within the school. Data from walkthroughs (including remote learning observations), products of PLC work from teams in the building, and teacher evaluation procedures are a regular aspect of these weekly meetings.

Jai meets formally with her two School Improvement chairs at least every two weeks for thirty minutes to an hour before or after school. In addition to these meetings, they have conversations at least weekly on an informal basis in the halls. Discussions center upon implementation of the School Improvement Action Plan, as well as specific tweaks that need to be made. Specifically, "just-in-time" learning for the staff—learning needs that are immediate—are discussed to ensure that monthly staff development sessions and staff meetings are meeting the most pressing professional learning needs of staff.

Even though the School Improvement chairs and building principal schedule meetings for every two weeks, it's difficult to maintain this schedule. Depending on the time of year—especially during certain sports seasons—meetings can get off-schedule. Still, Jai and the chairs work hard to keep in regular contact. They all know how important their work is, and even if only two of the three are able to meet, though not ideal, they still meet. Oddly enough, in a remote learning environment it is easier for them to hold this meeting sacrosanct.

Every month, the full School Improvement Team meets live or virtually to affirm the conversations of the chairs and building principal, as well as to bring the full Leadership Team up to speed. The most important tasks are those of detailed planning of staff development sessions and staff meetings—all according to the School Improvement Plan—and to receive updates from subcommittees. During the development of long-term plans, research on the most effective strategies and activities is the priority agenda item each month.

Subcommittees may meet monthly, quarterly, or each semester, depending on the specific tasks. The Reading Comprehension Subcommittee—a key priority of the plan—meets monthly to stay abreast of staff needs and propose specific plans for staff development sessions and staff meetings. The Problem Solving Subcommittee engages in the same activities as the Reading Comprehension Subcommittee, except its focus is upon systematically teaching students Problem Solving skills. The Communication Subcommittee meets quarterly to ensure ongoing and effective communication methods are being used between staff, students, parents, and the community. The

Wellness Subcommittee also meets quarterly and is not only focused on the physical well-being of students and staff, but also on social-emotional health. This subcommittee is particularly active around holidays, planning fun events for students and staff. There are several other subcommittees for the staff of eighty-plus teachers, but a few more notable ones are those of Technology Implementation, School Security, Data Organization, and College/Career Readiness.

Throughout all of the School Improvement work, every staff member is engaged at some level. Additionally, there are specific avenues for any concern and for considerable input on decisions that affect the entire school. Jai is ultimately responsible for all decisions, but all staff are provided opportunities, through the school improvement process and structures, to be involved in important decisions. Specifically, opportunities for input are provided, encouraged, expected, and ultimately implemented.

Teachers fully appreciate that there are regular opportunities for their voice to be heard. So-called "parking lot" conversations, where the real talk (especially griping) occurs after meetings, no longer occur. Teachers know where they can take their concerns, and are confident that concerns will be addressed. Further, teachers know that their ideas are valued, and in such a culture, more and better ideas flourish.

WANTING MORE?

Lambert, L. (1998). *Building Leadership Capacity in Schools.* Alexandria, VA: Association of Supervision and Curriculum Development.

Lambert, L. (2003). *Leadership Capacity for Lasting School Improvement.* Alexandria, VA: Association for Supervision and Curriculum Development.

Both of these texts are quick reads. The 2003 version is slightly updated from 1998. Linda Lambert provides examples of what the principles of the Lambert Framework look like in practice. Additionally, a self-analysis tool is provided as an appendix to reflect on the status of capacity-building in your organization.

Lezotte, L. (2005). "More Effective Schools: Professional Learning Communities in Action." In R. DuFour, R. Eaker, & R. DuFour (Eds.), *On Common Ground: The Power of Professional Learning Communities.* Bloomington, IN: National Educational Service.

Larry Lezotte's work has been around for ages and is incredibly consistent. The second iteration of his Correlates of Effective Schools directs itself toward building the capacity of students to improve their own learning. The seven correlates are simple and clear.

Marzano, R. J., Waters, T., & McNulty, B. A. (2005). *School Leadership that Works: From Research to Results.* Alexandria, VA: Association for Supervision and Curriculum Development.

One of the greatest and most influential researchers of our generation, Marzano, with colleagues from McREL, conducted a meta-analysis of research on school leadership. This text details the twenty-one principal behaviors associated with increased student achievement. An overview of the evolution of leadership theory over the past century, as well as a summary of the literature on magnitudes of change, is provided.

Self-Assess and Apply Your Knowledge

Use the following table to self-assess your knowledge on each of the statements. Note how you go about bridging any knowing-doing gap in order to make each one a reality.

	I need to learn more	I know this	I can teach others	What I DO to make this happen
Involve staff in making important decisions				
Provide opportunities for staff input on important decisions				
Encourage staff input on important decisions				
Expect staff input on important decisions				
Implement decisions based on staff input				
Engage *all* teachers in leadership roles				
Use a leadership team				
Differentiate between urgent and important activities				
Involve teachers in planning and implementing high-quality professional learning				

CHAPTER NINE

Principles of Student Learning

Elements of Principal Knowledge in Creating a Collaborative Workplace Environment for Teachers

To build a collaborative culture of professional learning, principals know and understand:

9. Aspects of student learning
    A. Curriculum
        1. What students should learn
        2. Alignment of daily objectives with grade-level outcomes to program goals
        3. A variety of Bloom's taxonomy verbs
        4. A variety of Kinds of Targets (KRiSP)
    B. Instruction
        1. Content and Pacing
            a. Daily lessons match curricular expectations
            b. Appropriate instructional level
            c. Pacing appropriate to maintain engagement
        2. Climate
            a. Appropriate discipline for orderly environment
            b. High expectations
            c. Efficient allocation of time
            d. Students on task and participating actively
            e. Structure for daily routines
            f. Many instructional strategies/tools
            g. Instructional strategies/tools matched to learning target(s)

C. Assessment
   1. Students' involved in assessment process
   2. Alignment between EWATR (Expectations, Written curriculum, Assessments, Taught curriculum, and what is Reported)
   3. Type of Evidence matches Kind of Target
      a. Teacher Observation: Knowledge, Reasoning, or Skill-level targets
      b. Selected Response: Knowledge-level targets
      c. Extended Written Response: Knowledge, Reasoning, or Product-level targets
      d. Performance Tasks: Reasoning, Skill, and Product-level targets

It may seem obvious to state, but at the risk of doing just that, the purpose of schools is student learning. Depending on who you talk to, or what you read, there may be differences in the perceived purpose of school. Whether a daycare for parents during the day, a place of socialization for children, or a site for athletic preparation, all of these potential secondary reasons for school pale in comparison to the true purpose of schools. Schools are a place for students to learn.

Given this fundamental and primary purpose of schools, it is a logical extension that the primary purpose of the principal is to ensure student learning. In order to ensure student learning, a principal must be knowledgeable about what is involved with student learning. In a nutshell, there are three basic building blocks of student learning, and these building blocks are true whether they are virtual or face-to-face. These foundational elements are the CIA of schooling: Curriculum, Instruction, and Assessment.

Though a principal must have a solid foundation of effective curricular, instructional, and assessment practices, it's important to keep this work in the context of leadership of the school in general. Keep in mind that "principals in PLCs are called upon to regard themselves as leaders of leaders rather than leaders of followers, and broadening teacher leadership becomes one of their priorities" (DuFour et al, 2005, p. 23). So while it is important for principals to be grounded in sound theory and practice, it is teachers who are the rightful instructional leaders in the building. The principal, in reality, will never assume the level of expertise in the specifics of curriculum, instruction, and assessment practices for every grade-level and content area that a classroom teacher will. Principals, really, are leaders of leaders.

While a principal doesn't need to, and really can't, know everything there is to know about the specifics of CIA for every content area, they must know what good curricular design, solid instruction, and assessment best-practice looks like. What's more important, though, is that they must be keenly aware of what is actually happening in the school regarding excellence in these areas.

Curriculum

The term "curriculum" is probably one of the least understood and most misused terms in education. For some, it means a textbook. For others, it means a sequence of courses. For others, it is the learning in which kids engage.

All, of course, have some measure of truth to them.

The most simple and clearest way to think of curriculum is to define it as "the what" of student learning. In the language of the Professional Learning Community movement, curriculum is the first question of PLCs: What do we want kids to know and be able to do?

So be clear about what students should know and be able to do by the end of a unit, course, year, or program. Whatever the endeavor, it really starts with large, broad goals that gradually narrow down into more and more levels of specificity, leading, ultimately, to outcomes at a daily or lesson level.

PHILOSOPHY/BELIEFS

At the foundation of quality curricular processes is the explicit statement of the beliefs that the school or system holds for 1) learners, 2) the process of learning, 3) the role of the teacher in learning, and 4) the importance of the content area. Succinctly (one page or less) writing down the collective beliefs of staff around these four questions will create a foundation for the next steps of the journey.

An effective and efficient process I have used to articulate our beliefs is to hand out 3 x 5 notecards to each member of the team or staff. Staff are then asked to respond to the four belief areas noted above based on their own thinking. Silent time, three or four minutes, is provided to write down their thinking.

After a short period of time, staff are then invited to pair up with another staff member to share and consolidate their beliefs around these four questions. Depending on the group, this typically takes anywhere from five to ten minutes.

The third step in the process is to have "pairs-square." Each pair joins another pair to, again, share their thinking and consolidate into one set of beliefs.

Finally, using chart paper or a blank document projected on a large screen, the facilitator captures the beliefs of each group while they are shared with the entire group.

After approximately thirty to forty-five minutes, the team will have a draft set of belief statements, and I believe it is important to just leave them as a draft for the time being. Over the course of a few meetings, it can be helpful to bring them back up and make revisions based on the need for clarity and/or additions or deletions. Of course, if the group doing this work is a representative group from the entire school or district, the representatives can take the draft to their colleagues and gather feedback in between each meeting. At some point, there will be a set of beliefs upon which all can agree and come back to regularly to ground themselves in why they are doing what they are doing.

The beauty of belief statements is that they can become a touchstone for effective practice later in the curriculum (or other) process. In my

PRINCIPLES OF STUDENT LEARNING 129

second or third year as a curriculum director, I led a review of Science curriculum materials. When we got to the point of looking at programs from publishers, individual members of the team referred back to the beliefs at several points to highlight how certain materials clearly did not align with the beliefs we had articulated earlier. Even though these materials were used by other nearby districts and even though they had flashy aspects to them, the mismatch between beliefs and what the materials asked students to do was glaring. Without me having to say a word to point this out, the team recognized this and moved on to other materials that were far better aligned and were effective in improving teacher practice and student learning.

CHART 6

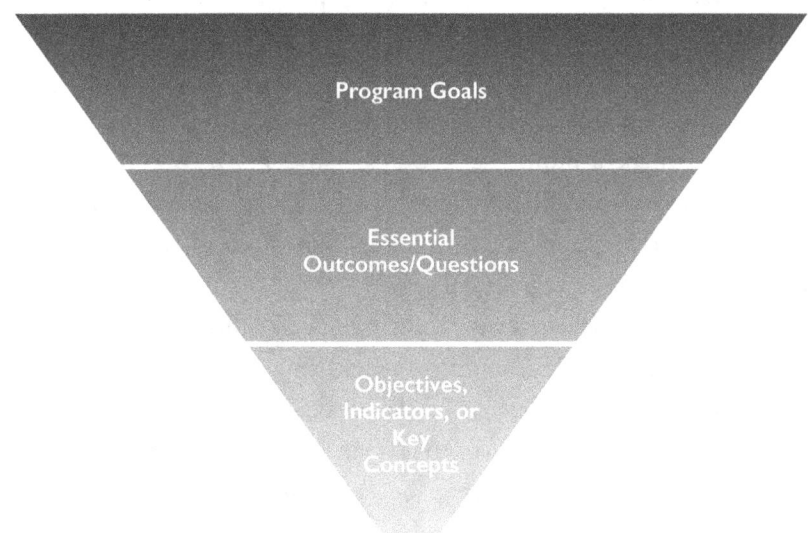

PROGRAM GOALS

Program goals are broad statements of intent by the end of a program. Simply ask yourself as an example, "What should a student know or be able to do as a result of studying Mathematics in our system when they graduate from high school?"

In addition to being broad statements of intent, program goals are student-focused. For example, "Students will use the principles of scientific inquiry to solve problems in their lives." Or, "Students will write independently to present clear ideas, descriptions, narratives, and arguments appropriate to a variety of situations, audiences, and purposes in the personal, academic, professional, and civic realms." Notice, in both of these examples, that the goals begin with "Students will..." statements.

For the sake of comparison, here are a few non-examples of program goals: "We will try to get kids to..." "Students will begin to..." "Hopefully students will..."

Recently I was facilitating a group of World Language teachers going through this process. They had articulated their philosophy and beliefs as a department around the notion of students becoming culturally literate. They wanted kids to be able to hold a conversation in another language, to seek opportunities to go to other countries, to appreciate the beautiful diversity of various cultures.

The program goals that they had developed aligned with these beliefs. They were broad statements of students being able to communicate in the target language, understand differences in cultures, and to seek out ways to learn about other cultures. But then we came to the annual, course-level essentials: these were focused on grammar. Student learning goals were centered on "preterite this" and "subjunctive that." There was absolutely no mention of effective communication or understanding of cultures. It was all about grammar.

What was remarkable about this experience was that the teachers themselves recognized this disconnect. There was no need for someone to come in and tell them how their essentials were wrong or bad or disconnected. Rather, through facilitating a conversation, starting with broad philosophy and working down to specific objectives, they came to the realization on their own that their essentials needed to be revised.

Grammar was not eliminated from their essentials. Instead, they made sure that their essentials were in alignment—and, I would contend, will be much more effective in getting kids to meet twenty-first century standards.

ESSENTIAL OUTCOMES/QUESTIONS

Essential outcomes or questions are more specific than program goals—but must align with and lead to the attainment of program goals. They are typically written at a grade and/or course level, and, like program goals, are student-focused. These also need to be written at a variety of levels of Bloom's Taxonomy.

OBJECTIVES, INDICATORS, OR KEY CONCEPTS

Some refer to these as objectives, others as indicators, others as key concepts. Regardless of what you call them, they are specific levels of knowledge, skill, reasoning, or product that students must acquire. These identify what students will learn as part of one or more lessons and also must support essential outcomes/questions, thereby supporting overall program goals.

As an example of an essential outcome with specific key concepts, consider the following for fifth grade Mathematics:

Essential:

Students will identify and demonstrate relationships among positive rational numbers.

Key Concepts:
Students will:

- Demonstrate an understanding of place value through millions and thousandths
- Compare and order whole numbers through billions place
- Classify a number as prime or composite
- Demonstrate how to write a whole number and a decimal number (to the thousandths) in standard, word, and expanded form
- Identify the factors and multiples of a whole number
- Compare and order decimals through the thousandths place
- Round whole numbers and decimals to any given place
- Recognize whether a fraction is in its simplest form
- Compare and order fractions
- Recognize and determine common equivalent fractions, decimals, and percents (3/4 = 0.75 = 75%)
- Find common denominators for fractions with unlike denominators
- Demonstrate equivalent decimals through the thousandths place (ex 0.5=0.50=0.500)

You'll notice that the larger essential is quite broad: positive rational numbers. Then the specific objectives are detailed—at the level of one or maybe several lessons.

Also, notice how the verbs are varied. In some cases, students identify. In other cases, students use their knowledge to do something (demonstrate how to write...). In still others, they are to make comparisons. This variety of verbiage associated with the outcomes is important for a quality curriculum.

PRINCIPLES OF STUDENT LEARNING

CHART 7

	Definition	Verbs
Knowledge	• Recall specific information • Remember previously learned materials	Arrange, Choose, Cite, Define, Describe, Duplicate, Fine, Identify, Label, List, Locate, Match, Memorize, Name, Order, Outline, Pronounce, Recite, Recognize, Relate, Recall, Repeat, Reproduce, Select, State, Tell, Underline
Comprehension	• Interpret communicated material without necessarily relating it to other material • Grasp the meaning of material	Classify, Convert, Defend, Describe, Discuss, Distinguish, Estimate, Explain, Express, Extend, Generalize, Give example(s), Identify, Indicate, Infer, Locate, Paraphrase, Predict, Recognize, Rewrite, Review, Select, Summarize, Translate
Application	• Use information in new or different situations • Use learned material in new and concrete or real-life situations	Apply, Arrange, Change, Choose, Compute, Construct, Demonstrate, Discover, Dramatize, Employ, Illustrate, Interpret, Make, Manipulate, Modify, Operate, Practice, Predict, Prepare, Produce, Relate, Schedule, Show, Sketch, Solve, Teach, Use, Utilize, Write
Analysis	• Break down information into parts • Break down material into its component parts so that its organization structure may be understood	Analyze, Appraise, Break down, Calculate, Categorize, Classify, Compare, Contrast, Criticize, Diagnose, Diagram, Differentiate, Discriminate, Dissect, Distinguish, Divide or Subdivide, Estimate, Examine, Experiment, Identify, Illustrate, Infer, Model, Order, Outline, Point out, Question, Relate, Select, Separate, Subdivide, Test
Synthesis	• Put pieces of information together into a new plan, idea, or product • Put parts together to form a new whole	Arrange, Assemble, Categorize, Collect, Combine, Compile, Compose, Construct, Create, Design, Develop, Devise, Explain, Formulate, Generate, Hypothesize, Integrate, Invent, Modify, Plan, Predict, Prepare, Propose, Rearrange, Reconstruct, Relate, Reorganize, Revise, Rewrite, Role-play, Set up, Summarize, Synthesize, Tell, Write
Evaluation	• Judge information according to criteria and offer supporting opinions and evidence • Judge the value of material for a given purpose	Appraise, Argue, Assess, Attach, Choose, Compare, Conclude, Contrast, Critique, Debate, Decide, Deduce, Defend, Describe, Discriminate, Dispute, Editorialize, Estimate, Evaluate, Explain, Grade, Judge, Justify, Interpret, Relate, Predict, Rate, Recommend, Select, Summarize, Support, Value, Verify, Weigh

CURRICULUM SUMMARY

Curriculum is the "what" of schooling: What do students need to know and be able to do? The daily work of students—key concepts, objectives, or indicators—must align with larger outcomes. Those larger essential outcomes/questions, then, must align with K-12 program goals. In this way, student learning from the micro level will support intended goals at the macro level. Finally, it is important to have a variety of verbs associated with "Student will..." statements to emphasize the variety of learning in which students must engage.

Instruction

Just as the most simple and clearest way to think of curriculum is as "the what" of student learning, instruction can be thought of as "the how." In the language of the Professional Learning Community movement, instruction is the third and fourth question of PLCs: What will we do when students don't know or are not able to do it? And: What about when they already know or can do it? Further, what will the teacher do if and when there is a mix in each classroom?

Of course, as noted earlier, the principal needs to be able to let the individual teacher and teams of teachers solve this for themselves, or to guide them through the challenges if they struggle. The building principal cannot and should not have all of the answers. Instead, you must be willing to help teachers find answers and resources to their questions of improving student learning.

So a solid understanding of instruction is needed in order to help teachers get students to the curricular targets. Instruction must be tailored to the best ways that students learn what they should learn by the end of a unit, course, year, or program. Just as with curriculum, instructional design must align with the outcomes at a daily or lesson level all the way up through the program level.

Instruction is highly complex. One teacher may have around thirty students in a classroom. Those thirty students are from different cultures, backgrounds, family histories, etc. Each and every one of them has different background knowledge, different vocabularies, and different life experiences. They all see with unique perspectives, and have individual perceptions of reality. Yet the job of the teacher is to get them all to a common end: the stated curriculum. Getting this done in the environment of a classroom is no easy task; it's highly complex. And in a virtual environment the barriers and challenges are magnified.

Nonetheless, there are certain observable behaviors that leadership should expect when in a classroom while conducting walkthroughs or observing in a virtual environment. These "Essential Skills Observable in Classroom Instruction" (Glatthorn et al., 2012) can be categorized as 1) Lesson content and pace, 2) Climate, and 3) Assessment. Each of these categories can be then broken down into specific "look-fors" when you are observing instruction. There are lots of these look-fors, and you will never see all of them, especially at first. You'll focus on the most important instructional skills, and, little by little, make an impact in improving instructional practices. As you do more and more observing you will get better and better at it.

> Essential Skills Observable in Classroom Instruction
> 1. Lesson content and pace
> 2. Climate
> 3. Assessment

LESSON CONTENT AND PACE

The attributes of lesson content and pace are threefold in nature. First, the content for lessons must directly relate to the curriculum and be at an appropriate level for students. In some ways this is the "Goldilocks" of lesson content—not so low that it creates boredom or too high to induce zone-out. And related is the notion that the assessment methods match the content that students are to learn.

Second, the content must be presented to students in an understandable way. The teacher must be clear about not only the content, but how they are conveying the content to students. Neither is sufficient without the other.

As a real-life example, I'm guessing most of us have had the unfortunate experience of being in a class where the instructor was a genius in their field but they couldn't convey the information to students if their life depended on it. On the other hand, some may have seen the equally unfortunate scenario of an outstanding teacher who has amazing pedagogical skills but who doesn't have the content knowledge of their subject matter. Both of these examples illustrate how both content and instructional strategies are important.

Finally, the teacher must pace instruction well. Great teachers do not go too fast. Neither do they go too slow. Rather, they vary their tempo depending on the content, the "feel" of the classroom and students, and a host of other factors. In essence, they read the "temperature" of the classroom and vary the tempo so that it is constantly changing and students are ever-engaged.

Lesson Content and Pace
1. Content alignment and appropriateness
2. Understandable—clarity of what students are learning and how it is taught
3. Pacing—not too fast and not too slow

CLIMATE

Classroom climate, according to Glatthorn et al., can be divided into seven different areas, though I have combined two into one and made it six areas: 1) Appropriate discipline, 2) High expectations, 3) Efficient allocation of time, 4) Students on task and participating actively, 5) Structure for classroom work, and 6) Use of instructional strategies.

A disciplined environment for student learning is essential for instruction to be effective. This does not mean that the teacher is Gestapo-like; some of the absolute best learning environments are the loudest classrooms in the building. Rather, there is an environment that is safe for students, and not just physically safe; there is also an environment where students are socially and emotionally accepted so they can take risks, make mistakes, and learn from their errors. This culture of learning in the classroom is the foundation for high-quality instruction.

If the culture of the classroom is the foundation for instruction, high expectations for students are the framework for that instruction.

Students will rise (or fall) to the teacher's (or your) expectations. Whatever you expect, students will meet. So have high expectations, unwaveringly high expectations—and hold your staff accountable for having high expectations for learning and their learners.

I have heard it said that a silver bullet of learning is time on task. This is not to say that we should necessarily have kids in school for more hours or days. What we should have is highly efficient use of the time that we already have kids in class. It just makes sense that the more time kids spend learning, the more they will learn. Hence, it is absolutely essential that instructional time is efficiently used to ensure that curriculum-related instruction is maximized.

As a few specific examples of wasted time, consider the following: How much time is wasted on watching movies that don't directly relate to content? Or maybe movies relate to the content, but effective instructional practices aren't used in conjunction to maximize learning? Or how many all-school announcements are made over the PA system that disrupt learning? Or how many classrooms have excessively lengthy transitions at the beginning or end of the day, or between subjects, or even between activities in class? These are all simple, but widespread, examples of wasted time in classrooms.

There are at least two ways to think of effective use of instructional time: use all the time and engage all the kids. Some people speak of "bell-to-bell" learning: from the moment the bell rings (or for the very best, before the bell rings as students are entering the classroom), kids are learning. And that learning continues right up until (and many times beyond) the end of the class. What's more, during the instruction, every kid is engaged. They are reading, writing, or talking about the content. They are absorbed in learning. They are on task the entire class period or day.

Classroom rules and procedures are a critical aspect of creating a healthy climate for student learning. This structure of rules and procedures provides a framework for student learning, and helps with ensuring a maximal use of time. Specific examples of organizing structures include the use of review, providing overviews, specifying student learning objectives (including stating them in student-friendly terms), providing clear directions, summarizing, and ensuring that assignments are relevant.

The sixth aspect of climate is that of the use of instructional strategies. The subject of a great deal of research in the past couple of decades, instructional strategies and their use is the crux of high-quality instruction. Here are a few questions to ask yourself when observing instruction:

- **What instructional strategies are being used?** Categories of instructional strategies include (Marzano, Pickering, and Pollock, 2001):
    - Identifying Similarities and Differences
    - Summarizing and Note Taking
    - Reinforcing Effort and Providing Recognition
    - Homework and Practice
    - Nonlinguistic Representations
    - Cooperative Learning
    - Setting Objectives and Providing Feedback
    - Generating and Testing Hypotheses
    - Cues, Questions, and Advance Organizers
- **What activities are being used by students to engage in the learning?**
- **What group structures are being employed by the teacher?**
    - Individual
    - Small Group
    - Cooperative Group
    - Large Group
- **Are the instructional strategies, activities, and group structures appropriate for the objective(s)?**
- **Does the teacher respond to student needs?**
- **Do the practices reflect sound learning theory?**

A thorough examination of these questions would fill one or more books by itself. Indeed, entire books do! One example is provided at the end of this chapter. The intent of this chapter is to give you a general idea of and structure for thinking about instructional practices that every principal should know.

> Climate:
> 1) Appropriate discipline,
> 2) High expectations,
> 3) Efficient allocation of time,
> 4) Students on task and participating actively,
> 5) Structure for classroom work, and
> 6) Use of instructional strategies

Assessment

In many ways, the term "assessment" has become synonymous with testing—and even connotes large-scale, standardized testing. But the true use of high-quality assessment in the classroom cannot be farther from that interpretation. Rather, high-quality assessment is happening every minute of every day, by both the teacher and the student, punctuated by moments of formal assessment—and highlighted, if you will, by state or national tests to measure program effectiveness.

> High-quality assessment is happening every minute of every day, by both the teacher and the student, punctuated by moments of formal assessment—and highlighted, by state or national tests to measure program effectiveness.

Assessment, very simply, is asking yourself, "How do I know when students know or can do what the curriculum calls for?" Remember that curriculum is "the what" of learning. Instruction is "the how." Assessment, then, is how we know that kids have actually learned.

Chappuis et al. (2012) distinguish between assessment OF learning and assessment FOR learning. Both are necessary components of high-quality education, though one has a far greater impact on improving student learning than the other.

Assessment OF learning occurs at the end of learning experiences. It is that formal test, or project, or performance that says to the teacher, the District, the state, or the feds either, "Yes, I have learned it." or, "No, I don't get it." Assessment OF learning is, simply put, a measurement OF learning. It does not increase learning—by itself, it *won't* increase learning. All it does is tell us the extent of the learning.

Because of the state and national focus on testing, assessment OF learning is the reason for the current connotation of assessment being a bad thing. People think of a test, standardized with bubbles and #2 pencils (or a computer with multiple-choice answers), as a one-size-fits-all assessment that is limited, at best. And they are correct.

But assessment FOR learning occurs throughout the learning of the student. It informs the teacher about student progress so that learning can be adjusted. It doesn't simply say what is and is not learned, but rather informs how much more learning on a given objective, indicator, or key concept is needed FOR more learning. It is inFORmative, about student progress, not just a summary of "Do you get it or not?"

The true test of assessment FOR learning, though, is not judged by the inFORmation provided to the *teacher*. The true test of assessment FOR learning is the extent that the assessment inFORms the *student's* learning. This is the litmus test: Do the assessments inFORm the student's learning? Does it drive corrections to past errors? Does it motivate further learning?

ASSESSMENT MATCH

Alignment, alignment, alignment.

Aside from understanding the difference between assessment OF and FOR learning, alignment is the most important thing to know about quality assessment. So what is alignment?

Alignment is when our Expectations for student learning match what is Written (the curriculum), which matches what is Assessed, which matches what is Taught, which matches what is Reported (grading practices). This alignment of EWATR leads to clarity for teacher and learner and facilitates high-quality instruction that improves student learning and achievement.

Expectations
align with what is
Written
which align with what is
Assessed
which align with what is
Taught
which align with what is
Reported

In regards to aligning Written curriculum with what is Assessed, Stiggins et al. (Chappuis et al, 2012) again provide excellent counsel. I think of it in three simple steps:

1. Clear targets
2. Appropriate assessments
3. Useful reporting

The first step of high-quality assessment is making sure that we have clear learning targets. This relates back to the curriculum aspect of instruction from earlier in this chapter—are our objectives, indicators, or key concepts clearly identified for students (and is the teacher using these to plan and drive their instruction)?

Assuming that clear learning targets are in place and that they are at an appropriate level of rigor and relevance (see the *Wanting More?* section to further your understanding of rigor and relevance), we turn to appropriate assessments.

Let's be clear: multiple-choice assessments are not appropriate assessments for all learning targets. As a matter of fact, they may not even be appropriate for a majority of learning targets.

So how do you know whether a multiple-choice assessment is appropriate or not?

You KRiSP it. You take the learning target and KRiSP it: Is it a Knowledge, Reasoning, Skill, or Product target? Here are some simple definitions of each:

> **Knowledge Targets** tend to be **factual** and often include verbs like **Know, List, Name, Identify, Recall**, etc.
>
> **Reasoning Targets** tend to involve the **application of content** to the real-world and often include verbs like **Predict, Infer, Classify, Hypothesize, Compare, Conclude, Summarize, Analyze, Evaluate, Generalize**, etc.
>
> **Skills Targets** are **performances** that must be **demonstrated and observed** (heard or seen)
>
> **Product Targets** call for a student to **create a product**.

Once we know the KRiSP status of a learning target, we then take a look at the available Types of Evidence. Just like there are four kinds of learning targets, there are four Types of Evidence: Teacher Observation, Selected Response, Extended Written Response, and Performance Assessment. These four types of evidence are on a continuum moving from most *informal* to most *formal*.

Teacher Observation / Informal Checks for Understanding

Ongoing assessments used as part of the instructional process. These assessments provide feedback to the teacher and the student. They are not typically scored or graded. Examples include:

- Teacher questioning
- Observations
- Examining student work
- Think-alouds

Selected Response / Quiz and Test Items

Familiar assessment formats consisting of simple, content-focused items that

- Assess for factual information, concepts, and discrete skill
- Use selected-response (e.g., multiple-choice, true-false, matching) or short-answer formats
- Typically have a single, best answer
- May be easily scored using an answer key or machine
- Are typically secure (i.e., items are not known in advance)

Extended Written Response / Academic Prompts

Open-ended questions or problems that require the student to think critically, not just recall knowledge, and to prepare a specific academic response, product, or performance. Such questions or problems

- Require constructed responses to specific prompts under school and exam conditions

- Are "open," with no single best answer or strategy expected for solving them
- Often require the development of a strategy
- Involve analysis, synthesis, and evaluation
- Typically require an explanation or defense of the answer given and methods used
- Require judgment-based scoring based on criteria and performance standards
- May or may not be secure
- Involve questions typically only asked of students in school

Performance Tasks

Complex challenges that mirror the issues and problems faced by adults. Ranging in length from short-term tasks to long-term, multi-staged projects, they yield one or more tangible products and/or performances. They differ from academic prompts in the following ways:

- Involve a real or simulated setting and the kind of constraints, background "noise," incentives, and opportunities an adult would find in a similar situation (i.e., they are authentic)
- Typically require the student to address an identified audience (real or simulated)
- Are based on a specific purpose that relates to the audience
- Allow students greater opportunity to personalize the task
- Are not secure: The task, evaluative criteria, and performance standards are known in advance and guide student work (Chappuis et al, 2012)

Knowing the KRiSP status of a learning objective drives the Type of Evidence necessary to inform the student and teacher about the learning. So this is how you know whether or not a multiple-choice assessment is appropriate. The following chart from Chappuis et al. (2012) displays how the two concepts interact with each other with KRiSP in the left-hand column and Types of Evidence across the top.

CHART 8
Links Among Kinds of Targets and Types of Evidence

Kind of Target	TYPE OF EVIDENCE			
	Teacher Observation (Checklist)	Selected Response (Quiz/Test)	Extended Written Response (Prompt, Rubric, Checklist, Criteria)	Performance Assessment (Rubric, Checklist, Criteria)
Knowledge Mastery	Can ask questions, evaluate answers, and infer mastery—but a time-consuming option.	Good match for assessing mastery of elements of knowledge.	Good match for tapping understanding of relationships among elements of knowledge.	Not a good match—too time-consuming to cover everything.
Reasoning Proficiency	Can ask student to "think aloud" or can ask follow-up questions to probe reasoning.	Good match only for assessing understanding of some patterns of reasoning.	Written descriptions of complex problem solutions can provide a window into reasoning proficiency.	Can watch students solve some problems and infer reasoning proficiency.
Skills	Strong match when skill is oral communication proficiency; not a good match otherwise.	Not a good match. Can assess mastery of the knowledge prerequisites to skillful performance, but cannot rely on these to tap the skill itself.		Good match. Can observe and evaluate skills as they are being performed.
Ability to Create Products	Not a good match.	Not a good match. Can assess mastery of knowledge prerequisite to the ability to create quality products, but cannot use to assess the quality of products themselves.	Strong match when the product is written. Not a good match when the product is not written.	Good match. Can assess the attributes of the product itself.

Once you know the KRiSP status of a learning target, you can then identify the Type of Evidence that will be the best match for that learning target. For example, Knowledge-level targets are good matches for Selected Response and Extended Written Response—but not good for Teacher Observation or Performance Task. On the other hand, Skill-level targets are not good matches for Selected and Extended Written Response, but excellent for Teacher Observation or Performance Task.

The most common mismatch that I see is that we have identified Reasoning or Skill-level learning targets but try to assess them with Selected Response items—mostly because these are easy to score (or grade). But this is a bad match!

You, as the building principal, must be able to understand the differences between the Kinds of Targets and Types of Evidence. You must be able to help teachers to see the differences. You must be able to see the differences in action. And you must be able to help move teachers to better match the Kind of Target with the Type of Evidence that they will use.

Finally, as noted by Chappuis et al., reporting of assessment results must match. Assessments OF learning are what we typically think of reporting: quizzes, tests, report cards, parent-teacher conferences, and state tests. And these assessments are helpful when they align (EWATR—Expectations align with what is Written align with what is Assessed align with what is Taught align with what is Reported).

Take this thinking about assessments one step further: making sure that students understand what *they* are learning. Recall that with assessment FOR learning, the litmus test is whether or not it inFORms the *student* about their learning and further motivates them to keep on learning.

Do students, on a day-to-day basis, understand what they are learning? Are the results of the assessments FOR learning used *by students* in the classroom? Do these assessments inFORm their learning? Does it drive their learning? Are the results visible (while maintaining FERPA compliance) in the classroom? Ultimately, can students tell you what they are learning?

Assessment FOR Learning
- Does the student understand what they are learning, each and every day?
- Do the assessment and results inform the student?
- Does it drive the student's learning?
- Are results visible in the classroom?
- Can students tell *you* what they are learning?

ASSESSMENT SUMMARY

There are two broad categories of assessment: assessment OF learning and assessment FOR learning. These broad categories are appropriate for all levels of students. Assessment OF learning measures how much learning has occurred in a summary fashion. Assessment FOR learning is used to inFORm both the teacher and the student about their progress toward meeting learning targets. The litmus test for telling the difference between the two categories of assessment is whether or not the assessment inFORms the *student* about their progress.

Alignment of Expectations, Written curriculum, Assessments, what is Taught, and the Reporting (EWATR) of student learning are paramount to effective instruction. Alignment also includes having clear learning targets (KRiSP) and matching appropriate assessment types to those learning targets. Finally, effective reporting of student learning means that those reports are based on the learning targets that are aligned with EWATR.

CIA Summary

The primary purpose of the principal is to ensure student learning. In order to ensure student learning, a principal must know what is involved with student learning. The three basic building blocks of student learning are the CIA: Curriculum, Instruction, and Assessment, although a principal should never mistake themselves as needing to know all of the specific details associated with every curricular area.

In PLCs, principals are called upon to regard themselves as leaders of leaders rather than leaders of followers. As such, broadening teacher leadership becomes one of your priorities. And while you need to be grounded in sound theory and practice of CIA, it is teachers who are the rightful instructional leaders in the building.

You don't need to, and really can't, know everything there is to know about CIA. Nonetheless, you must know what good curricular design, solid instruction, and assessment best-practice looks like—whether face-to-face or virtually. What's more important, though, is that you are keenly aware of what is actually happening in your building's classrooms (live and/or virtually).

WANTING MORE?

Chappuis, J., Stiggins, R. J., Chappuis, S., & Arter, J. A. (2012). *Classroom Assessment for Student Learning: Doing It Right—Using It Well (2nd ed.).* Boston, MA: Allyn & Bacon.

An excellent step-by-step guide to assessment literacy. Whether studied individually, in learning teams, or as an entire faculty, this guide will increase the ability of staff to effectively and efficiently assess student learning: both of and for. The text comes with a number of tools to assist with the learning, and there is also a text for leaders that may be of interest:

Chappuis, S., Stiggins, R.J., Arter, J., & Chappuis, J. (2006). *Assessment for Learning: An Action Guide for School Leaders,* 2nd ed.

https://leadered.com/rigor-relevance-framework/

The terms of rigor and relevance have gained almost cult-like status where people use these terms without necessarily understanding them. The International Center for Leadership in Education (ICLE) coined the terms, and because of this have the most succinct and useful definitions of the terms—not to mention tools to assist with the full understanding and use of rigor and relevance. Their website will be a helpful resource for those wanting to learn more.

Marzano, R. J., Pickering, D., & Pollock, J. E. (2001). *Classroom Instruction that Works: Research-Based Strategies for Increasing Student Achievement.* Alexandria, VA: Association for Supervision and Curriculum Development.

An oldie but a goodie, this book provides a categorization of research-based instructional strategies into nine categories ranging from Identifying Similarities and Differences to effective Homework practices. It details the research behind the strategies and specific actions that teachers and schools can take to implement them. For the most part, they are instructional strategies that most teachers already use, just not with enough frequency, depth, or fidelity to significantly impact student learning. This text will assist with all three.

Self-Assess and Apply Your Knowledge

Use the following table to self-assess your knowledge on each of the statements. Note how you go about bridging any knowing-doing gap in order to make each one a reality.

Curriculum

Curriculum	I need to learn more	I know this	I can teach others	What I DO to make this happen
Curriculum is what students should learn				
Daily objectives must align with course or grade-level outcomes				
Course or grade-level outcomes must align with program goals				
A variety of Bloom's taxonomy verbs must be used when devising daily objectives, course or grade-level outcomes, and program goals				
A variety of kinds of targets (KRiSP) must be used in daily objectives, course or grade-level outcomes, and program goals				

Instruction

Instruction	I need to learn more	I know this	I can teach others	What I DO to make this happen
The content of daily lessons should match curricular expectations				
Content must be an appropriate instructional level for students				
The pacing of content must be appropriate for students in order to maintain engagement				
Appropriate discipline must be used to maintain an orderly environment				
Teachers must have high expectations for student achievement				
Teachers must efficiently allocate time				
Students must be on task and participating actively				
The teacher must structure the daily classroom routines				
There are many instructional strategies/tools that can be used to get kids to the curricular expectations				
The teacher uses a variety of instructional strategies/tools that are matched to the curricular expectations and learning needs of students				

Assessment

Assessment	I need to learn more	I know this	I can teach others	What I DO to make this happen
Students must be involved in the assessment process				
There must be alignment between EWATR (Expectations, Written curriculum, Assessments, Taught curriculum, and what is Reported)				
The Type of Evidence must match the Kind of Target				
Teacher Observation is a good assessment for Knowledge, Reasoning, or Skill-level targets				
Selected response assessments are good at measuring Knowledge-level targets				
Extended Written Response is good at measuring Knowledge, Reasoning, or Product-level (when a written product) targets				
Performance Tasks are a good match for Reasoning, Skill, and Product-level targets				

CHAPTER TEN

Principles of Change and Sustainability

Elements of Principal Knowledge in Creating a Collaborative Workplace Environment for Teachers

To build a collaborative culture of professional learning, principals know and understand:

10. Principles of change and sustainability
    A. Principles of sustainability
    B. Consensus should be built
    C. Persistence is needed
    D. Meaningful change is extremely hard
    E. There is a difference between adaptive and technical barriers

"If you want to make enemies, try to change something."
Wilson, 2013

Of course, change isn't quite that simple. It does, however, definitely have the potential to irritate a few people; meaningful change is extremely hard. And it is even harder in a remote learning environment where the challenges of building relationships are even more difficult.

So how can you minimize disruptions to your change efforts while maximizing the improvements to student learning that you are seeking?

The other nine chapters of this text walk you through the elements necessary to create a collaborative workplace environment for teachers.

Now we will explore a few additional concepts that you need to know in order to effectively lead change, regardless of the specific change.

Lead Change—Not Manage Change

First of all, it's important to understand that while you can lead change, you cannot manage it. You cannot control it. You cannot sell it. You cannot use your natural charisma or woo to get it done (remember from Chapter One that charisma does not lead to long-term leadership success). You cannot foresee where the change will take you. You cannot necessarily predict who will react in which ways. And you cannot direct the change like a control tower operator directing planes at an airport.

This is because change—if it is truly to impact student learning—is incredibly hard.

Instead of trying to control change, you have to lead change. You create the conditions for change to occur. You build the capacity of the people in your organization to make change happen. You develop your own capacity to tolerate ambiguity—remember that this is the hardest, yet most rewarding, work. In short, you *do* the other nine Elements of Principal Knowledge.

Because change is incredibly difficult (if it is meaningful), that means that you can't give up easily. Change is absolutely necessary for growth to occur. And so is persistence. You must be inventive, be persistent, and hold high expectations. Meaningful changes that improve student learning take time—especially those that are systemic and systematic. So be patient. And persist in your efforts, for there will be opposition. Be okay with it, and don't panic.

Finally, in thinking about the difficulty of change and your role in leading change, you must be aware of the difference between what Heifitz (1994) calls adaptive and technical barriers. Adaptive issues are those that don't necessarily have right or wrong answers. They require collaboration and skillful insight into human psychology. Adaptive issues, almost always, involve the interaction of people.

As Lambert (1998, p. 9) stated, "Leadership is about learning that leads to constructive change." Leadership must be about facilitating learning and seeking out adaptive solutions to adaptive problems—not seeking that silver bullet. Humility and continuous improvement are keystones. And these attitudes of learning and humility, coupled with the skills necessary to convey these, are foundational to leading change.

Technical barriers, on the other hand, tend to be relatively simple (especially compared to adaptive barriers). They many times do have right or wrong answers. Even though technical barriers can be simpler, don't be fooled. Without a doubt, technical problems can absolutely sink a change initiative. In order to maximize the effectiveness of a change effort, staff have to be keenly aware of the difference between technical and adaptive difficulties. And the difference isn't always so easy to distinguish.

For example, a school was undergoing a one-to-one initiative where laptop computers were purchased for every student. Some of the difficulties encountered involved the availability of bandwidth, the distribution of computers, the use of rental agreement documents, and staff training. You may know well the barriers that must be overcome in distributing computers to every student in a building.

To take one aspect, the availability of bandwidth seemed to be an issue. At first glance, this was thought to be a technical problem—simply add bandwidth and the problem vanishes. But after further examination, it became clear that this problem didn't have such easy solutions. For the more bandwidth that was added, the more bandwidth was used.

Clamping down on student use of the computers wasn't effective, either—after all, wasn't the purpose of getting the computers into students' hands the whole point of going one-to-one?

Instead, it required education and consensus-building on the part of students. Students needed to be taught appropriate and inappropriate uses of the computer. They needed to be guided to better use their electronic devices. Teachers needed to be taught how to appropriately respond to student misuse of the laptops. And they also needed to be guided in how to assign meaningful learning activities that resulted in appropriate use of the computers to improve student learning.

The problem, though initially perceived as technical and fairly simple, wasn't technical or simple at all. It was quite complex, and many schools still struggle with this adaptive challenge because they confront it as a technical one.

No matter what the change initiative, there will be barriers. You must be able to discern the difference between adaptive and technical problems, and then address them accordingly.

When I first became a high school principal, I tried to sit back and observe as much as possible. One of my observations on the very first student day was the lunch line. Students walked down one side of a six-foot-wide hallway and picked up their silverware and milk. They then turned around and walked back—in the middle of the hallway—to get in line for lunch. The line for lunch, of course, then turned back down the hall. So there were essentially three lines of students in a six-foot-wide space.

Needless to say, this didn't work. There was cutting between the lines, poking each other with forks and spoons, stealing of milk, and other nonsense. The three-lines-in-one scenario was just creating more problems than it was solving.

So what was the technical difficulty? I consulted with other lunch supervisors and we decided to move these items so that one line was formed. Interestingly enough, even this simple move had resistors! There were many reasons, according to these people, for leaving the system as it was. Fortunately, we made the change anyway, persevered through the resistance, and improved the lunch line for kids. The students probably never even noticed the difference in their behavior—but the adults sure did. Office referrals over lunch (and in the afternoon) plummeted and student behavior improved. This technical, management change was an important one.

Relationships, Relationships, Relationships

At the risk of belaboring a point discussed in Chapter One, let me highlight the absolute imperative of positive relationships with staff. Positive relationships are the *sine qua non* of change. Translated literally, this Latin phrase means "without which there is nothing." Without positive relationships, you will not effect change. And without effecting change, you will not improve student learning.

> Without positive relationships, you will not effect change. Without effecting change, you will not improve student learning.

Meaningful and long-term change will not be successful without positive relationships. Once you leave, if the changes are not systemic and systematic, the changes will leave with you. But with relationships built, you will see that the changes become embedded in the culture, become part of the organization (as opposed to driven by you), and have a better chance of enduring beyond your tenure.

Collaboration, built with positive relationships, leads to building consensus among staff. This consensus, then, leads to long-term change and improvements. The change doesn't become a flavor of the month, or the latest fad of the leader, or a mandate from above—but instead a change initiated by the members of the organization. It becomes a change understood by, led by, and driven by your leadership team. It becomes the will of the group.

> Collaboration leads to Consensus,
> which leads to Commitment,
> which leads to Long-term Change

Just because there is consensus doesn't mean that everyone will be onboard. Go anyway. The ship must sail.

Sustainability

The ultimate test of quality leadership is sustainability. What about the work of a leader endures beyond the tenure of the leader? For if our impact is only temporary, what impact have we truly had? Sustainability sees to the long-term impact of our work.

Hargreaves and Fink (2006) enunciated seven principles for sustainable leadership:

Sustainable leadership...
1. Creates and preserves sustaining learning
2. Secures success over time
3. Sustains the leadership of others
4. Addresses issues of social justice
5. Develops rather than depletes human and material resources
6. Develops environment diversity and capacity
7. Undertakes activist engagement with the environment

Some of these principles seem a little disconnected from education, so let's examine them a little more closely.

The first principle means that we, first and foremost, focus on learning. If we focus on learning, then achievement and test scores will take care of themselves. However, the reverse is NOT true: If we focus on test scores, achievement and learning will not necessarily happen.

The second principle says that we should focus on long-term success. Just as a gardener does not focus on one season or one harvest, so, too, in education must we have a long-term view. Results over not just one, two, or three years—but over five, ten, and twenty years are what really matter to student learning.

Sustaining leadership of others, the third principle, is really what the bulk of this book is about. Sustainable leadership is about building the capacity of others to do the work of leadership. For the building principal will likely move on—and the teachers will remain. And teachers need the capacity to improve the school. Leadership is about learning—not about designated positions of authority in the organization.

> **Sustainable leadership is about building the capacity of others to do the work of leadership. And leadership is about learning—not about designated positions of authority in the organization.**

The idea of addressing social justice in school leadership is an interesting idea. It means that sustainable leadership makes sure that efforts we take in schools will not undermine the work of other schools. For instance, we don't go about improving one school by shipping all of the low-performing students to a nearby school, or creating policies that restrict the entrance of those students. This hurts some kids, and is, quite frankly, immoral. Rather, sustainable leadership makes sure that the work of improving student learning is about improving the learning of *all* students—not just those in your school building, your district, your county, your state, or even our nation.

In the wake of raised consciousness around social justice issues, too, this idea takes on added meaning. How do we ensure that students are thinking of themselves as connected beings with each other and the planet? How do we empower students to make a difference in their own and others' lives? How do we guarantee that the mistakes of the past don't become replicated in the next generation—that we are, truly, carrying forward an ever-advancing civilization? How do we make sure that the result of learning isn't simply memorization, but a call to the betterment of ourselves and the world around us? These and other questions can assist us in thinking about sustainable leadership as it relates to social justice.

Developing human and material resources, too, seems like a no-brainer. However, how many times have we seen schools or districts take on a strategy of simply hiring more people to do the work—rather than building the capacity of those already in the organization to improve their practice? Hiring more people can very easily translate into a depletion of human and material resources, so we need to be selective in who we hire and that for which we hire. And we must make sure that one of our top priorities is building the capacity of our designated leaders to do their job more effectively and efficiently.

For example, whenever a person retires or leaves a school, it behooves us to think carefully about how to best maximize our human resources. Too many times we automatically go into hiring mode. But is this the best decision? It might be. But it might also be best to think about the organization as a whole, the people within the organization, the mission of the organization, and how to best access the expertise of the people in the organization to meet the mission. In most cases, it will likely be to hire a replacement. In some others, it won't.

The idea of environmental diversity, too, seems odd in a school leadership context. But Hargreaves and Fink (2006) make an interesting point on this front, as well. And that is that diversity in the environment is healthy and necessary. Diversity is also necessary in schools. Standardization of schools does not work. Standardization of classrooms does not work. Standardization of students does not work. What works is diversity, and a recognition that diversity is not only needed, but healthy.

This diversity manifests itself in diverse thinking and practices. It is important for designated leaders to encourage diverse thinking and not stymie those voices who provide differing views—and to even center those voices that have been traditionally marginalized and silenced. Additionally, it's important to encourage different practices—it is not healthy to have all teachers teaching the same thing, the same way, in the same minute of every day. Standardization is not healthy.

Finally, sustainable leadership takes on issues in a proactive way. Leaders interested in long-term change make sure that they are not simply compliant with district, state, or federal mandates. Rather, they work to change those mandates for the good of students. They funnel resources into being proactive to influence the debate and decisions that influence their schools. They don't sit idly by and allow themselves to be the fodder of policy-makers. But instead, they forge their own destinies.

Summary of Change

Change is hard.

If that's not an understatement, I don't know what is.

Change requires hard work. It requires collaboration. It requires patience and persistence.

Change requires positive relationships and building consensus among your stakeholders. It necessitates an understanding that you can lead change, but you cannot manage it. As such, it requires that you increase your tolerance for ambiguity. And it requires the ability to tell the difference between adaptive and technical barriers and then choose actions based on which type of change you face.

WANTING MORE?

Fullan, M. (2020). *Leading in a Culture of Change (2nd ed.).* San Francisco, CA: Jossey-Bass.

The leader in educational change theory and practice, Michael Fullan details five principles for leading change. A fairly quick read, *Leading in a Culture of Change* will help you develop an understanding and appreciation of what it takes to successfully lead positive change in your school.

Self-Assess and Apply Your Knowledge

Use the following table to self-assess your knowledge on each of the statements. Note how you go about bridging any knowing-doing gap in order to make each one a reality.

	I need to learn more	I **know** this	I can teach others	What I DO to make this happen
Meaningful change is extremely hard				
Consensus should be built				
Persistence is needed				
There is a difference between adaptive and technical barriers				
Learning first—then achievement and test scores will follow (not vice-versa)				
Our focus should be on long-term learning				
Successful change develops the capacity of others				
Improvements should not harm students in other settings				
Develop capacity—not necessarily hire more people				
Diversity, not standardization				
Be proactive, not reactive, to policy				

CHAPTER ELEVEN

A Call to Action

This text is based on the assumption that there is not just a knowing-doing gap in improving our schools but a knowing gap. In order to do, we must first know. I cannot change my behavior unless I know what to do differently. Thus, a knowing gap.

Even still, knowing is not enough. One of the key differences between leaders and great leaders is that they not just know, but they do. Unfortunately, there are too many of us who don't know, and therefore can't do. Now that you know, you can do.

There are actions that others *could* do to improve student learning. There are steps that school districts *should* do. Of course, there are things that parents *might* do. This book is about what a principal *can* do. This is about *your* sphere of influence, where *you* can have the biggest impact. This book highlights what a principal must know in order to create a collaborative workplace environment for teachers. Now there is no excuse—let's close that widespread knowing-doing gap.

Now that you know, use this text as a touchstone to come back to and remind yourself of that which you must do. Use the stories to generate additional ways of creating a collaborative community. Use the checklists to self-assess and push yourself further, as well as provide them to others to assess where you and the school are on the journey. Take action. Turn that knowledge into results—for both staff and students. And as you take action, you will learn through your doing.

Organizations in every field seem unable to change existing knowledge, research, and advice into meaningful action. Let's be one of the first fields to close this persistent gap. As my firstborn would say when he was about two years old, "Let's do it!" Our children, every single one of them, deserve nothing less.

Bibliography

Barth, R. (2005). "Turning book burners into lifelong learners." In R. DuFour, R. Eaker, & R. DuFour (Eds.), *On Common Ground: The power of Professional Learning Communities*. Bloomington, IN: National Educational Service.

Blanchard, K., Meyer, P. J., & Ruhe, D. (2007). *Know Can Do! Put Your Know-how into Action*. San Francisco: Berrett-Koehler.

Chappuis, J., Stiggins, R. J., Chappuis, S., & Arter, J. A. (2012). *Classroom Assessment for Student Learning: Doing It Right—Using It Well (2nd ed.)*. Boston: Allyn & Bacon.

Collins, J. (2001). *Good to Great: Why Some Companies Make the Leap...And Others Don't*. New York: HarperCollins.

Costa, L., & Garmston, R. J. (2002). *Cognitive Coaching: A Foundation for Renaissance Schools*. Norwood, MA: Christopher-Gordon.

Council of Chief State School Officers. (2008). *Educational Leadership Policy Standards: ISLLC 2008*. Washington, DC: Author. Retrieved on September 12, 2009, from http://www.ccsso.org/publications/details.cfm?PublicationID=365.

Covey, S. R. (1990). *The 7 Habits of Highly Effective People: Powerful Lessons in Personal Change*. New York: Simon & Schuster.

Darling-Hammond, L., & McLaughlin, M. W. (1995). "Policies that support professional development in an era of reform." In M. W. McLaughlin & I. Oberman (Eds.), *Teacher Learning: New Policies, New Practices*. New York: Teachers College Press.

Davenport, T. H. (2005). *Thinking for a Living: How to Get Better Performance and Results from Knowledge Workers*. Boston: Harvard Business School Press.

Deering, A., Dilts, R., & Russell, J. (2003). "Leadership cults and culture." *Leader to Leader, 28*, 31-38.

Deming, W. E. (1986). *Out of the Crisis*. Cambridge, MA: The MIT Press.

DePree, M. (1989). *Leadership Is an Art*. New York: Bantam Doubleday Dell.

Drucker P. F. (1999). *Management Challenges for the 21st Century*. Oxford: Butterworth-Heinemann.

DuFour, R., & Berkey, T. (1995). "The principal as staff developer." *Journal of Staff Development, 16*(4). Retrieved on June 19, 2009, from the National Staff Development Council website, http://www.nsdc.org/news/jsd/dufour164.cfm.

DuFour, R., DuFour, R., Eaker, R., & Many, T. (2006). *Learning by Doing: A Handbook for Professional Learning Communities*. Bloomington, IN: Solution Tree.

DuFour, R., Eaker, R., & DuFour, R. (2005). Recurring themes of Professional Learning Communities and the assumptions they challenge. In R. DuFour, R. Eaker, & R. DuFour (Eds.), *On Common Ground: The Power of Professional Learning Communities*. Bloomington, IN: National Educational Service.

Duhigg, C. (2016, February 25). What Google learned from its quest to build the perfect team. *The New York Times*. Retrieved from https://www.nytimes.com/2016/02/28/magazine/what-google-learned-from-its-quest-to-build-the-perfect-team.html.

Dumas, C. (2010). *Building Leadership: The Knowledge of Principals in Creating Collaborative Communities of Professional Learning*. (Doctoral dissertation, University of Nebraska, Lincoln, Nebraska). Retrieved from https://digitalcommons.unl.edu/cehsedaddiss/33/

Easton, L. B. (Ed.). (2015). *Powerful Designs for Professional Learning (3rd ed.)*. Oxford, OH: Learning Forward.

Eastwood, K., & Lewis, K. S. (1992). "Restructuring that lasts: Managing the performance dip." *Journal of School Leadership, 2*(2), 213-224.

Freire, P. (1970, 1993). Chapter 3 In *Pedagogy of the Oppressed*. London: The Continuum International Publishing Group. Retrieved from http://www.historyisaweapon.com/defcon2/pedagogy/pedagogychapter3.html.

Fullan, M. (2020). *Leading in a Culture of Change (2nd ed.)*. San Francisco: Jossey-Bass.

Fullan, M. (2003). *The Moral Imperative of School Leadership*. Thousand Oaks, CA: Corwin.

Garmston, R. J. and Wellman, B. M. (2016). *The Adaptive School: A Sourcebook for Developing Collaborative Groups*. Lanham, MD: Rowman & Littlefield.

Glatthorn, A. A., Boschee, F., Whitehead, B. M., Boschess, B. F. (2012). *Curriculum Leadership: Strategies for Development and Implementation* (3rd ed.). Thousand Oaks, CA: SAGE Publications, Inc.

Gronn, P. (1996). "From transactions to transformations: A New world order in the study of leadership." *Educational Management & Administration,* 22(1), 7–30.

Hargreaves, A., & Fink, D. (2006). *Sustainable Leadership.* San Francisco: Jossey-Bass.

Heifetz, R. A. (1994). *Leadership Without Easy Answers.* Cambridge, MA: Harvard University Press.

Kouzes, J., & Posner, B. (1996). "Seven lessons for leading the voyage to the future." In F. Hesselbein, M. Goldsmith, & R. Beckhard (Eds.), *The Leader of the Future.* San Francisco: Jossey-Bass.

Lambert, L. (1998). *Building Leadership Capacity in Schools.* Alexandria, VA: Association of Supervision and Curriculum Development.

Lambert, L. (2003). *Leadership Capacity for Lasting School Improvement.* Alexandria, VA: Association for Supervision and Curriculum Development.

Langer, G. M., Colton, A. B., & Goff, L. S. (2003). *Collaborative Analysis of Student Work: Improving Teaching and Learning.* Alexandria, VA: Association of Supervision and Curriculum Development.

Learning Forward. (2011). *Standards for Professional Learning.* Oxford, OH: Learning Forward.

Learning Forward. (2012). *Standards into Practice: School-based Roles. Innovation Configuration Maps for Standards for Professional Learning.* Oxford, OH: Learning Forward.

Lezotte, L. (2005). "More effective schools: Professional learning communities in action." In R. DuFour, R. Eaker, & R. DuFour (Eds.), *On Common Ground: The Power of Professional Learning Communities.* Bloomington, IN: National Educational Service.

Lieberman, A., & McLaughlin, M. W. (1995). *Networks for Educational Change: Powerful and Problematic.* In M. W. McLaughlin & I. Oberman (Eds.), *Teacher Learning: New Policies, New Practices.* New York: Teachers College Press.

Little, J. W. (1990). "The persistence of privacy: Autonomy and initiative in teachers' professional relations." *Teachers College Record,* 91(4), 509-536.

Marzano, R. J., Pickering, D., & Pollock, J. E. (2001). *Classroom Instruction that Works: Research-based Strategies for Increasing Student Achievement.* Alexandria, VA: Association for Supervision and Curriculum Development.

Marzano, R. J., Waters, T., & McNulty, B. A. (2005). *School Leadership that Works: From Research to Results*. Alexandria, VA: Association for Supervision and Curriculum Development.

Marzano, R. J. (2007). *The Art and Science of Teaching: A Comprehensive Framework for Effective Instruction*. Alexandria, VA: Association for Supervision and Curriculum Development.

Mullen, C. A., & Hutinger, J. L. (2008). "The principal's role in fostering collaborative learning communities through faculty study group development." *Theory Into Practice, 47*(4), 276–285.

Murphy, C. U., & Lick, D. W. (2005). *Whole-faculty Study Groups: Creating Professional Learning Communities that Target Student Learning*. Thousand Oaks, CA: Corwin.

Murphy, J., Smylie, M., Mayrowetz, D., & Louis, K. S. (2009). "The role of the principal in fostering the development of distributed leadership." *School Leadership and Management, 29*(2), 181–214.

National Association of Elementary School Principals. (2008). *Leading Learning Communities: Standards for What Principals Should Know and Be Able to Do (2nd ed.)*. Alexandria, VA: National Association of Elementary School Principals.

National Study of School Evaluation. (2006). *Breakthrough School Improvement: An Action Guide for Greater and Faster Results*. Schaumberg, IL: National Study of School Evaluation.

Newmann, F. M., & Wehlage, G. G. (1995). *Successful School Restructuring: A Report to the Public and Educators*. Madison, WI: Center on Organization and Restructuring of Schools, Wisconsin Center for Educational Research, University of Wisconsin.

Pfeffer, J., & Sutton, R. I. (1999). "Knowing 'what' to do is not enough: Turning knowledge into action." *California Management Review, 42*(1), 83–108.

Schmoker, M. (2005). "No turning back: The ironclad case for Professional Learning Communities." In R. DuFour, R. Eaker, & R. DuFour (Eds.), *On Common Ground: The Power of Professional Learning Communities*. Bloomington, IN: National Educational Service.

Sparks, D. (2003). "Change agent: An interview with Michael Fullan." *Journal of Staff Development, 24*(1), 55-58.

Sparks, D. (2007). *Leading for Results (2nd ed.)*. Thousand Oaks, CA: Corwin.

Stone, D., Patton, B., & Heen, S. (1999). *Difficult Conversations: How to Discuss What Matters Most.* New York: Penguin Books.

Whitaker, T. (2003). *What Great Principals Do Differently: Fifteen Things That Matter Most.* Larchmont, NY: Eye on Education.

Wilson, W. (6, July 2020). "Woodrow Wilson." Retrieved from http://www.searchquotes.com/quotation/If_you_want_to_make_enemies,_try_to_change_something./279218/

Glossary

Collaboration—Teachers working together in the shared pursuit of improving professional practices that improve student learning.

Collaborative workplace environment—Closely related to the definition of collaboration; a school where teachers work together in the shared pursuit of improving professional practices that improve student learning is a collaborative workplace environment. Specifically, this involves the development of leadership skills of the entire staff, the distribution of power, and the general building of the capacity of teachers. Most importantly, the collaborative workplace environment must be focused on improving student learning.

Declarative knowledge—Blanchard et al. (2007, p. 2) describe declarative knowledge as "information [one has] picked up from books, audios, videos, and seminars." For these purposes, it also includes knowledge obtained from sources such as mentors, significant role models, and others. The Council of Chief State School Officers (2008) adds to the definition abilities, awareness, information, and other accumulated knowledge based on field and classroom experience.

Designated leadership—Those who are invested with specific roles identified with that which is typically considered leadership responsibilities. At the building level, designated leadership refers to building principals.

Job-embedded professional learning—"Learning activities that occur during work hours and that support instructional needs" (Mullen & Hutinger, 2008).

Leadership—In brief, Lambert's five tenets of leadership frame this definition:

1. Leadership is not trait theory; leadership and leader are not the same.

2. Leadership is about learning that leads to constructive change.
3. Everyone has the potential and right to work as a leader.
4. Leading is a shared endeavor.
5. Leadership requires the redistribution of power and authority. (Lambert, 1998, pp. 8-9)

In other words, the work of leadership can and should be done by the masses.

Procedural knowledge/skills—Building on the work of Blanchard et al. (2007), procedural knowledge, or skills, is defined as the use or application of declarative knowledge.

Professional learning—Learning that teachers engage in as part of their work. Typically, educators think of workshops as the primary mode of professional learning. Professional learning is any learning in which a teacher engages—from workshop to study group, designing lessons to analyzing assessments and their results, reading journal articles and reflecting on their practice.

Professional learning community—A community of professionals (i.e., teachers and administrators) who work together (collaboratively) using specific structures and processes to improve the learning of all students. Many models abound, including Whole-Faculty Study Groups, the DuFour model, Collaborative Analysis of Student Work, and others.

Processes—Process is the how of professional learning. It involves the parameters and tools for the work of the school. Protocols are an example of a specific process.

Protocols—Protocols are step-by-step procedures for engaging in work as teams.

Structures—Closely related to systems, structures are necessary for putting systems into place. Structures like department-level configurations or teams based on common students are typical structures in schools.

Systems—A system is an organized collection of parts working together to accomplish a goal or goals. Typically, educators think of schools as systems. There are also systems at the school, department, and classroom level.

Acknowledgments

This manuscript started its journey to becoming a book in 2012, inspired by the urging of my beloved wife, Dawn. I made significant progress, but then it languished in the land of almost-written books—until the spring of 2020 when our individual and collective lives were thrown into tumult. It is no exaggeration to say that if it weren't for Dawn's continued encouragement to get this to press, it would still be in that never-seen land.

Diel and Kalim, our two college-aged boys, have always been incredibly supportive through thick and thin. Their patience with me as a father and human being has always meant a lot, and I look forward to seeing their service to humanity come into full bloom.

Ernie and Sandy Dumas, my parents, and Danelle Stith, my sister, always have my back, and Jamie, my brother who passed away, always showed up when we needed him and is now closer than ever from the next world. Of course, my brothers from another mother, Daryoush and Saadat Hosseini, have always challenged my thinking and helped me become a better person. And I have informally adopted Hal and Jubi Maggiore as family.

Martha Bullen guided me through the publishing process, Christy Collins created beautiful designs, and David Aretha made incredibly detailed and helpful edits. Joellen Killion, Lee Jenkins, Jennifer Abrams, Scott Blum, Shaeley Santiago, Mary Morton, Lana LaSalle, Craig Kautz, Nancy Vincent Zinke, and Barbara KV and Rick Johnson provided helpful feedback on the content of the manuscript. And Todd Whitaker's support of this project and his terrific foreword are appreciated beyond words.

While my dissertation provided a theoretical foundation for this book, my practical experiences since that time refined my thinking and provided many of the stories. The staff at Gibbon graciously brought me in and taught me how to be a leader. Together, we opened a new building and chapter for the school and community, and our time together is held fondly in my heart.

Craig Kautz hired me in a high-poverty, high-diversity district. The Superintendent's Cabinet meetings were a highlight of this team: Donna Moss, Trent Kelly, and Jeff Schneider are all dearly treasured souls. Denise Behrends and Sara Johnson are the most amazing administrative assistants, and their willingness to ask tough questions and push my thinking was always appreciated. Our building principals, the frontline of building a collaborative culture, challenged me and partnered in improving our culture to the point of having multiple National PLC Models: Ann Auten, Cathy Cafferty, Jay Opperman, Montessa Muñoz, Lawrence Tunks, Amy Kelly, Jason Cafferty, David Essink, Irina Erickson, Cara Kimball, Tom Szlanda, and Charla Brant. Numerous instructional coaches, teachers, and teacher leaders all taught me invaluable lessons that I carry with me to this day.

The team at Ames was incredible, and even though I was focused on elementary, my secondary colleagues (Brian Carico and Yonas Michael) were no slouches. Jeff Hawkins, Anthony Jones, and Darcy Cosens were tremendous partners. The CIA Team—Mary Morton, Vonda Junck, Shaeley Santiago, Nicole Kuhns, Dan Andrews, Deani Thomas, Jessica Sharp, and Linda Jones—are incredibly knowledgeable and talented, and it was pure joy to serve with them each and every day.

Finally, the team with whom I have had no other peer in my years in education and for whom words cannot express my appreciation for your kindness and support through a year like no other: Kristen Barber, Lana LaSalle, Steve Flynn, Justin Jeffs, Kristi Mixdorf, and Sue Lawler. Thank you.

About the Author

DR. CHAD DUMAS is an educational consultant, international presenter and award-winning researcher whose primary focus is collaborating to develop capacity for continuous improvement. Having been a successful teacher, principal, central office administrator, professional developer and consultant in a variety of school districts, he brings his passion, knowledge, and skills to his writing and speaking as he engages participants in meaningful and practical learning. By seamlessly weaving engaging stories with education research and offering hands-on tools with clear processes, Chad offers readers and audiences useful knowledge and skills they can implement immediately.

The results of Chad's work speak for themselves. One district was identified as "Persistently Lowest Achieving" upon his arrival, and within a few years — by applying the principles of this book — multiple schools were recognized as National PLC Models for improving student learning. Chad has served on and led accreditation visits for Cognia around the United States and world, presented nationally and internationally, collaborated with school boards, intermediate service agencies, state departments of education, and professional associations, and trained as an agency trainer for Adaptive Schools.

To learn more about Chad's work and to contact him about consulting or speaking, please visit www.NextLearningSolutions.com.

www.ingramcontent.com/pod-product-compliance
Lightning Source LLC
Chambersburg PA
CBHW072155100526
44589CB00015B/2238